FUNNY
ABOUT
THAT

FUNNY
ABOUT
THAT

BY JOHN GOULD

Drawings by Consuelo Eames Hanks

W·W·NORTON & COMPANY
New York   London

The text of this book is composed in Palatino
Composition and manufacturing by
The Maple-Vail Book Manufacturing Group

First Edition

Library of Congress Cataloging in Publication Data

Gould, John, 1908–
Funny about that / John Gould.
p.   cm.
1. Maine—Social life and customs—Humor.   I. Title.
PS3513.0852F86   1992
813'.52—dc20   91–17731

ISBN 0-393-03049-0

W.W. Norton & Company, Inc., 500 Fifth Avenue, New York, N.Y. 10110
W.W. Norton & Company, Ltd., 10 Coptic Street, London WC1A 1PU

1 2 3 4 5 6 7 8 9 0

For My Favorite Jones Girl
Kay Dornbusch

Contents

Peter Partout's Page

Dear Mr. Editor; It was I who asked Dr. Gould if he knew whatever became of Shine Fauchette, and perhaps I should have kept my big mouth shut.

(Signed) Peter Partout—Peppermint Corner

FUNNY
ABOUT
THAT

1 Funny About That

Clevie and Theo Bickford used their garage and Ford sales agency as the base for numerous related and unrelated ventures, and 'twas said the Bickford Boys could lay their hands on more ready money sooner than anybody else in town. They had a finger in about everything but instead of looking the part of wealthy men they went about in overalls and frocks, felt boots and rubbers, and one time Clevie put on a suit with necktie and went to a funeral and nobody knew who he was. One day, back during War No. 2, Clevie drew me aside one morning to say, "Bring in your cans and leave 'em." He meant my five-gallon gasoline cans for tractor fuel.

The desk-soldiers who fought that war so valiantly in Washington gave the farmers plenty of ration stamps for tractor gasoline, but there was no way we could get gasoline. If a transport of gasoline came to the Bickford Garage, the village people would spot it, word would run around, and everybody would line up and drain the Bickford pump before the farmers could arrive with their cans. Clevie accordingly told the villagers that he was pumped dry when he still had gasoline, and in the dead of night he would go to the garage, line the farmers' cans up in the dark, and take care of us. He would feel for the cap on a can, stick the nozzle in, and wait for five dings on the pump. We grew a lot of beans and shipped a lot of eggs and milk, and thanks to Clevie we won the war, although we did deprive the patriotic villagers of a few joyrides.

So I took my three tractor cans down to the Bickford Garage and left them, and that night Clevie came to carry all the empty cans from the back room in the garage, line them up on the sidewalk, and make ready to pump. There was, at that time, great fear in Washington that Hitler was about to send bombers to obliterate our little town, so we had a big blackout. Clevie couldn't turn on any lights. And we also had an alert Civil Defense Unit equipped with helmets and gas masks which practiced diligently and was ready on an instant's notice to take stations and protect us. Clevie got things ready and stuck the nozzle in the first can. Just then the Civil Defense people called for a practice alert, and the town's fire siren went off in an extended wail that curdled milk in the outskirts and called everybody to stations. Clevie, listening to dings, got to three when the siren let go.

George Pelley lived just up the street, and he jumped from bed, pulled on his pants, and started for his post at the gate of the woollen mill. As he ran along, fumbling at his belt and trying to fasten the strap on his helmet, he came abreast of Clevie's array of gasoline cans on the sidewalk and there was a tumultuous collision. Cans went in all directions, George did likewise, and Clevie shouted instructions that were lost in the wail of the siren. George picked himself up and continued on to his post, where presumably he did his part in the exercise prescribed. After a few minutes the siren blew an all-out, and George started home.

By this time Clevie had rounded up his dispersed cans and had them lined up by the pump again and was about to insert the nozzle. This time Clevie was able to call a warning, and he went in the dark and got George by the hand and led him past the array of cans, but George was curious and wanted to know what was going on. Clevie told him to march home and keep his trap shut. In the end George won the CD meritorious award for faithful performance at air raid drills, but Clevie was the one we farmers credited with winning the war.

One Saturday morning after peace was restored I went to the

garage to get my cans filled, and Clevie was just getting into his pick-up truck to go somewhere. He came to pump and I said, "Where're you bound?" He said he was going up to Wayne to pay off a crew that was cutting pulpwood and firewood, and I said if I had a lunch packed I'd go along for the ride. "No need," said Clevie, "we get there just at noonin', and they feed."

I went along for the ride. Clevie said he and Theo (he always said T'eo) had picked up some acreage and had some Frenchmen from Rumford stripping the lot. Mostly pulp, but some hardwood and a few good sawlogs. The last two or three miles of road into the camp were conjectural, but Clevie found them and the pick-up managed. We came to a considerable building close to a brook, and the cook was standing in the open door. The camp was big enough to sleep a dozen men—cook, cookee, and ten choppers—and serve also as cookshack. Clevie called, "Mornin!"

"Bonjour," said the cook.

I hadn't been expected, so now the cookee set another place—an even dozen, since the cook and cookee wouldn't sit. The inside of the camp was rich with the effluent of a bubbling pot on the stove. Anybody knowing anything about a woods camp could foretell a stew. Finest kind! Pies, cakes, cookies, bread, and other with-its were plentiful on a counter and the camp seemed to be the right place for the time being. Clevie took a strongbox and a folder of papers to the end of the table and began looking at timesheets. The cook stirred the pot. Then the cookee put a hammer to the come-and-get-it and went immediately to the stove and began dipping from the pot. As he started to dip, the crew was already at table. Every man by now had his milk and sugar in the teacup and butter on his first slice of bread.

Clevie and I took our places and got nods from everybody, and the stew exercises began. The stew was as good as it smelled, and would embellish the menu at any table in the world. Stews should be loose, and this one had ample juice. The stew meat had been reduced to proper gobbits and rightly sautéed with maple syrup before any of the concomitant necessities had been introduced. Onions, potatoes, carrots, all such had been inserted in the correct order and at the precise time, with knowing hand and purposeful intent. The cook stood with his arms folded and listened to the men as they ate, as any virtuoso enjoys deserved applause. The cookee kept dipping.

After the men were paid and Clevie had given the cook the check for supplies, the crew started for home in Rumford and the weekend. The cook would follow after the clean-up, but the cookee was watchman and would stay in camp. Clevie and I could go home.

I shook hands with the cook and complimented him on the excellence of his beef stew.

"Porcépic!" he said.

Clevie told me as we rode along home that it saved him considerable money at the butcher's. The porcupine is largely nocturnal and likes to spend the daylight perched high in the top of a pine tree. Now and then the choppers would bring down such a pine, and after the tree crashed to the ground the poor porky would stagger out, dazed and shaken, and wander away to find a new perch. After a certain exposure to such bouncing a porky gets punch-drunk. The choppers find it amusing that a porky who staggers out of one tree will usually go directly to the one that is due to be felled next, and will climb to reach the highest limb. But a downed porky is easy to subdue, and Clevie's cook was kept well supplied with meat for his unequalled porky stews.

It's the only time I ever ate porcupine.

Now and again Clevie would tell me he'd been up to Wayne for payday and the cook had asked for me, and then one day he said the lot was stripped and the operation was finished. He and Theo would let the land go to the town for unpaid taxes, and that was commonly done in those days. Then, a few years later, Clevie said, " 'Member that camp up to Wayne?"

"Turned out it warn't never on our land. We thought it was, but it was eighty feet over the line. It had a good roof, so it stayed tight, and we heard somebody bought it and moved it to the lake and made a cottage from it. T'eo and I went to look, and there it was, a real stylish cottage. I had Lou Jack go up and size things up, and somehow he managed to get thirteen-hundred out of the thing. Which suited us. Lou took seven-fifty for his law fee, and that was all right, too. T'eo and I never had more'n a hundred and fifty in it, and we only gave two hundred for the land. Funny how some things work out."

2 The Smartest Dog

The smartest dog I ever met was a Redbone hound called Scamper. He was a shade bigger than a beagle, but not much, and he belonged heart and hide to Buddy Russell, who was proprietor of Maine's prestigious summer resort, the Kennebago Lake Club nine miles in the woods beyond Rangeley village. Scamper was a rabbit dog, and was so sharply trained that no other scent beguiled him. In the evening, when guests were sitting about the big lobby listening to the guides' tall tales and yawning until bedtime, Buddy and Scamper would be over in the far corner on a stuffed chair, sound asleep. Buddy's head would be tipped back and Scamper would be stretched along his thigh, muzzle on Buddy's knee. Both of them had been up since 4:30 that morning—Buddy to check the kitchen and make ready for the day, and Scamper to begin his morning exercise with the rabbits.

In the winter, when Kennebago was icebound and the guests were back home, Buddy would go into the puckerbrush with

Scamper to do some pot hunting. Scamper never paid any heed to deer, foxes, bobcats, and any other residents of the region, but he'd take off after a snowshoe rabbit and bellow like the bulls and banshees in all the books. Maine rabbits are not really rabbits; they are the variable hare that is brown in summer and white on snow, and they have huge hind legs that let them jump forty feet or more. Scamper kept them humping. In the summer hunting bunnies was out of season, so as official rabbit hound of the Kennebago Lake Club Scamper could chase only the resident rabbits that were tame around the camp. The "camp" was a considerable hotel complex of a big lodge, dining room with kitchen, quarters for the help, and over a score of log cabins where guests had their rooms. The resident rabbits were wild, but guests would entice them to friendship with shreds of lettuce brought from the kitchen. They weren't afraid of anything, including Scamper, but they kept Scamper amused by loping along ahead of him if he got close. Every so often Scamper and the rabbits would rest. This interminable chase amused the guests, and it never approached tragedy since no hound has ever been fast enough to catch a snowshoe rabbit that is in good health and in his right mind. Scamper wouldn't have known what to do if he'd caught one.

So it happened one particular summer, along in August, that a Mr. and Mrs. Tecumseh Millington from the very Main Line applied for accommodations and were assigned to Antlers, which was considered the favored log cabin at Kennebago. It is appropriate that Mr. and Mrs. Millington came from Philadelphia, since all the best foils in Maine woods stories are from that estimable place. They arrived at Rangeley air strip by private plane, and Buddy met them with his convertible to drive them into camp. At first sight, the Millingtons seemed all right to Buddy, except that they had two dogs—huge and handsome boxers that came on leashes and bubbled all over Buddy as they were introduced. Well, just one big boxer can be overpowering to somebody who keeps a slim little beagle himself. They calmed down some after a couple of laps around the hangar, and then Buddy got them in the front seat with him and he started into the woods. The Millingtons remarked on the weather, observed that the air was clean and the scenery agreeable, and the two boxers slobbered all over Buddy for the nine miles of the road. Buddy pulled up at the lodge, and the two boxers boiled out to take over Kennebago.

The front seat of that convertible rightly belonged to Scamper, and now he came from the lobby to greet Buddy and to make love to him, and from the porch he got a whiff of boxer and he put on the brakes. He stuck his nose in the air and then advanced to give Buddy a good sniff, and he stiffened in disgust. But Scamper composed himself and as befitted the good hound that he was he advanced to welcome the two boxers to Kennebago. They were paying customers. During that afternoon the boxers investigated everything, and had their ears patted by all the guests, and Scamper played second fiddle to them until by supper time he was a mess. But he kept his feelings to himself, and it was only Buddy who noticed. Buddy said, "Nose out of joint, eh, old fellow? Well, never mind!"

The next morning Scamper bounded forth and suggested to the two boxers that they might enjoy a few rounds with his bunnies, and when the guests came to the lodge for breakfast they were pleased to see how well Scamper and the boxers were hitting it off. The boxers paid no heed to the rabbits, but Scamper was trying and he kept one on the run and kept looking back to see why the boxers didn't help him. After breakfast, when the guests came out of the lodge, Scamper and the boxers were silent—fact is, they were gone. Not a dog in sight, and Scamper's bugle tooted nary a note. The rabbits were right up by the porch, chewing grass.

Well, Scamper had taken those two out-of-state summer dogs on a woods romp, and after he got them over on the far side of Spotted Mountain he contrived to put himself on the other side of a tree, and he came back to Kennebago Lake Club by the long way around, and he left those two boxers to become Babes in the Wood. Come supper time Scamper was in the lounge waiting for Buddy to finish eating and come to sit down, and as the saying goes butter wouldn't melt in his mouth. He was up on Buddy's knee and sound asleep when Mr. and Mrs. Tecumseh Millington came in to ask if anybody had seen Tom and Jerry. (That's the boxers).

No, nobody had seen Tom and Jerry. Nobody recalled seeing them since some time that forenoon. They roused Buddy to ask if he had seen Tom and Jerry, and while Buddy came to and showed some interest, Scamper kept sleeping. That evening the search consisted of a chorus by the guests, up and down, calling to Tom and Jerry. But in the morning the guides all turned out, and the fish-and-game plane flew in a couple of wardens to organize a search. Four days later Tom and Jerry were found over towards Tim Pond, about ten hound-dog miles from Kennebago Lake Club, and Tom was so weak he had to be carried. The Millingtons returned to Philadelphia, and once again Scamper was King of the Hill.

3 Beevo Saves the Play

B eevo, my first dog, had greatness thrust upon him for one brief encounter, but was otherwise without redeeming features except for snuggling at my back in bed. This was an asset on cold winter nights, but in hot July it was not. He would go to bed before me and arise after me, so I was never in want for a cozy bedfellow, but other than that Beevo was never cited for useful deeds. He was the stupidest dog of all dogs.

Beevo was no good whatever as a watchdog, for his amiable disposition caused him to welcome tramps in at the front door and escort them upstairs. My mother once found such a tramp taking a bath in the family tub, Beevo watching with great interest. Beevo had no notion of defending the castle, and as he was afraid of cats he would hide if one loped from the bushes towards our hen pens. Being a somewhat beagle, he should have had some talent at the hunt, but he was timid in the woods and went to great lengths to avoid any woods instruction. But he'd walk halfway to school with me and meet me halfway home, and Beevo and I never made any unkind remarks about each other. His one big moment, up to the time he ran away and never came back, was when he went on the stage and became an actor.

Beevo came to me gratuitously. Dave Longway, who lived up on the Durham Road, had a beagle bitch of unusual prowess, and her deeds on the bunny track were almost legendary. If Dave invited anybody to go into the woods with him along with Dumpling, anybody was sure to accept. Dumpling was classic, and had a way of pausing at just the right spot so the rabbit would stop to sit up on his hind legs and look about, wondering whatever became of Dumpling, and this was always right where the hunter was waiting. Dumpling was an artist. But Dumpling met a wayfaring man somewhere in the vicinity, and in due time was delivered of a generous litter of pups that were noticeably part beagle and part wayfarer. When Dave came out from the house that morning to chore up, he looked at Dumpling's brood and spoke to her with disapproval so that she blushed. When the pups were weaned Dave made a crate and shipped them collect to a pet shop in Boston.

The oddity of Dumpling's pups was the legs. The eight little devils were cute as could be otherwise, and everything about them was true beagle in the upper areas. Dumpling had put her mark on them, and they had beautiful ears, good heads, proper bodies, and just right tails. But the legs—they might have come from a giraffe. And this was bad, because the basic beauty of a beagle is the shortness of the legs—beagle legs should keep the pooch down to earth and consistently moderate when on the scent. A dog that keeps a rabbit going too fast will be the one whose legs are too long. So Dave packed the eight pups into the crate and nailed on the cover and turned everything over to Lee Soule. Lee was the local railway express agent, and he stuck the crate on the milk train that afternoon and hi-ho-and-away Dumpling's brood was headed for Boston.

When the crate got to the pet store in Boston, the proprietor looked to see what he had, and having seen he nailed the cover back on the crate, and with a black marking crayon he wrote across the top: "REFUSED—RETURN TO SENDER." Even in Boston, a long-legged beagle is hard to sell. When the crate came back, Lee Soule got in touch with Dave Longway, and Dave said, "Who, me? There must be some mistake." So that afternoon my father spoke to me thus, saying, "If you'd like a nice little pup, go down to the railroad station and pick one out." Lee Soule, as express agent, had instructions to dispose of unclaimed items, and he'd sent word around that pups were available—free. I came home with Beevo in my arms, and he was my first very-own dog, and he was a slob.

Beevo's bright moment as a Thespian came when he was maybe four years old. We—I—had long since realized he wasn't good for anything except to snuggle at my back, so it meant a good deal when he was invited to appear in a play. I suppose not too many today can go back and relate to the wandering players who would come into the small towns with entertainment and culture. The town house, the Pythian lodge hall, the sail loft at the shipyard would become a theatre, and our bereft situation would be enhanced. *East Lynn* was still being played and other favorites of that stripe, and so was *Uncle Tom's Cabin*. We had heard of motion pictures, but so far none had appeared.

Uncle Tom's Cabin, like the circus, had a street parade to urge desire on the populace, but never such a good one as the circus.

Limited to the cast and backstage hands, the *Uncle Tom's Cabin* parade gained length when everybody walked single file and spaced out at thirty paces, and the only animals were the bloodhounds. Doc Rockwell, the late vaudeville comedian, traveled with an *Uncle Tom's Cabin* troupe in his earlier days, and he said he got the part because he could blow a tin whistle in the parade. The circus parade had its magnificent steam organ, but *Uncle Tom's Cabin* had Doc Rockwell. He marched behind Simon Legree, who had the bloodhounds on leashes, and the dogs were trained to put on a show of ferocity—although bloodhounds are really sweet and gentle. Doc said the dogs never got fed until after the parade, so they strained on the leashes all the way. Doc said he always played "The Stars and Stripes Forever," which made the bloodhounds strain all the more. The tune, he thought, hurt their ears. In the play, Doc did three different characters, but not all at the same time, and in a pinch had done Little Eva. But my Beevo was before Doc Rockwell's time.

It was in 1920 that Beevo played in *Uncle Tom's Cabin*. The man come to our house and rapped on the door to introduce himself to my mother as the manager of such-and-such players, and he said he would like to have her attend his play. He handed her two tickets. Mother said she guessed not, but he said the tickets were free, and she said, "Oh, that's different." Thus he came to broach his problem, which was serious.

He said his crate of bloodhounds, due to arrive that morning by railway express, had been set off by mistake at Yarmouth Junction and had gone on the up-train of the Canadian National Grand Trunk to, as far as he knew, Montreal. The depot telegrapher was trying to intercept the crate at Island Pond, Vermont, but there was no way they could have the dogs back in time for the parade and the matinee. He had been told in the village that we had a dog that he might borrow in the meantime.

Mother coaxed Beevo from under the stove, and after he stood for a few moments and waked up he wagged his tail vigorously at the strange man to demonstrate his warm affability. The man could see that Beevo was not likely to epitomize ferocity, but his ears did droop and he looked somewhat like a hound and the time was short and the need was great. So Beevo was cast as a bloodhound in *Uncle Tom's Cabin*. Before parade time the man was able to find two other dogs suitable for the stage, one of which was Lon Bubier's crack bobcat hound, a veteran of many woodland skirmishes that showed in the style of his ears. Lon's dog and Beevo were good friends in a nonprofessional way, but the third dog was a stranger to both. So Beevo marched in the parade, but Simon Legree had to keep pushing him with one foot. And he was in the play, too, and I was proud of him. He tagged at my heels as Mother and I walked home after the performance, and my mother said that considering that he was Beevo, any drama critic would have to concede that his histrionic talent was at least desultory.

Soon after that Beevo left me. We were in the swamp over towards the Marshal place, and Beevo was bugling in great shape until a stranger would think he was running a rabbit, and I had my .22 rifle but no bullets. That was the way to hunt with Beevo, because he was gun-shy. We had our lunch by the big pine tree, and after his piece of cake he jumped up and ran off in full cry. He kept on going, and he disappeared beyond the swamp and went over the hill and I never saw him again.

4 Real Amusing

The funniest, and stupidest, happening of the past half century is the New Hampshire presidential primary, and the record shows just one joke that ever came out of it—not counting the candidates. It's truly hard to believe, for this country needs more than anything else the big squelch for the presuming ass who thinks he's good enough to be President of the United States of America. They come to New Hampshire in flocks every presidential year and for some reason hitherto unexplained the granite-headed New Hampshire electorate accords them serious dignity. Here in Maine, every fourth year, we have to put up with this New Hampshire frivolity, and we don't deserve it.

New Hampshire, you see, doesn't have any television. Well, they have a station, but the topography, or geography, of New Hampshire sets up skips and a good part of the state is in valleys over the mountains, and the thing doesn't tune in. But here in Maine we have three good TV stations in the Portland area that boom into New Hampshire. One of them, WMTW-TV, channel 8, even has its transmitter atop Mount Washington, although the offices and studios are in Maine. So, since TV now makes the mare go, the New Hampshire presidential primary is actually fought out on Maine television, and we poor souls who don't give one hoot are captive to the whole prolonged show.

There's nothing like it anywhere in organized politics, or on television. We realize that our politics, and our TV, in Maine are as odd and comical as anybody's, but we keep things to ourselves and don't shove them down our neighbors' throats. When the New Hampshire primary pot begins to simmer, it always takes me by surprise. Well, the year in Maine has been good, as usual, and things are in hand. The wotsome garden was productive and I got the turnips threshed in good season and the onions bound in sheaves. The beans stacked harmoniously and winnowed out fine. Larder and freezer are goodied to the hilt. Taxes paid. Now let winter draw on! The last hunting season accident has been investigated and the victim duly reprimanded, and the evenings come early. Cooler weather, but a full woodbox by the cozy stove. Boots off, feet up, and the rocking chair agile. And now let us see what the television offers to lull the slack before supper. With three channels, we have good choice. "Family Feud," "Barney Miller," "Superior Court"—maybe "Merv Griffin," and sometimes another rerun of "What Price Glory?" All, of course, larded with the same repetitive commercials for Lilt, Tide, Polident, Crispies, cruises, and easy-come insurance about which no salesman will call. Excellent bland amusement to embellish the contented mind that is merely waiting for, ". . . chops are on the table!" So it surprises me when the mood of our mellow Maine and our innocent doldrum is punctured by the first burst of campaign bombardment aimed at the people of New Hampshire. What's that to do with me?

With dancing girls, fireworks, fanfare, brass bands, natty necktie, fancy forensics, and a toothy grin somebody I never heard of is assuring me he is the only man in the world equal to the task of running the country. I do it every time—I rise from my comfort with the assumption that our TV station has lost its marbles. Why me? Why us? Why Maine? Lulled as I am in the routine of composure, the sudden flamboyant political commercial is out of all context—Mother Goose has intruded in a Phi Beta Kappa exercise. But our Maine TV stations have not lost their marbles and they are taking in the dough, and they have astutely arranged an answering service to intercept me when I telephone to object. All three channels—6, 8, and 13—promised to leave notes on the managers' desks just as soon as they got back from the banks.

That first TV commercial of the New Hampshire season is followed by the spate, and from then until the votes are counted we Mainers spend considerable time on the back stoop throwing up. Unless you've lived in Maine during a New Hampshire primary, you couldn't know what we put up with. We long for news about Lilt, Tide, Polident, Crispies, cruises, and insurance about which no salesman will call. True, we have the intellectual pleasure of wondering why the people of New Hampshire have all gone crazy, and that's something, if not much.

The one joke that has developed out of the New Hampshire presidential primary is resurrected every fourth year and brought out as if fresh and new. As things build up, and more and more candidates appear to solicit New Hampshire's favor, it gets so that we folks in Maine lose track and things get fuzzy and dubious. You get the Ferrara pitch mixed up with the Glenn, and you wonder if peace in Miami hinges on abortions. Just who was it that wants to triple the SS payments? We don't have programs, and get the shortstop playing left field, sort of. So the story goes that one of the presidential candidates in the New Hampshire primary got on the wrong road one afternoon, and he drove across the state line into Maine—coming thus to our contented community of Gilead where the usual worthies were sitting by the stove in the store. He thought he was still in New Hampshire.

He came into the store with the affable optimism characteristic of the breed, stuck his hand forward heartily, and said, "Good afternoon, Gentlemen—I'm Walter Mondale, and I hope you all know I'm running for the presidency!"

"Eyah," said Henry Trauble. "We know—we was just sittin' here laughing 'bout that!"

5 The Buckeye Malfunction

Quite a jolt when I realized what a malfunction is. The news told me that the multi-million space probe had been called off because of a malfunction—*due* to a malfunction is what the man said, but who knows the language nowadays? I grew up with the simplistic presumption that a leaky faucet was a leaky faucet, and if we couldn't fix it with a wrench from the barn we could call Sears, Roebuck and the man would come Tuesday. I had the chills of a sudden when I realized what could

happen with a leaky faucet *up there.* Living out in the seques-
tered and deprived country makes most everybody handy, and
I reflected about that interplanetary malfunction and thought of
all the things I've fixed in my life without giving them a second
thought. Fix or make do. As a boy, I could take my Model T
apart and put it together, often with a few bolts left over, and
that was a good place to start. Times have changed, and now I
don't even know where the battery is, and it doesn't help a bit
to recall that my Model T didn't have any battery.

A persistent malfunction on the old farm had to do with the
Buckeye mower. We made hay when the sun shone, but only
after surmounting repeated malfunctions with the Buckeye. The
model I inherited had a four-foot cutter bar and was designed
for one horse. We took away the "sharves" and fitted a short
tongue, so we could hay with the doodle-bug tractor (first in
town) and this took two astronauts—one to drive the doodle-
bug and one to handle the Buckeye. We were a well trained
team, and if we encountered a malfunction we got off and took
care of it. The tractor was our own invention, in a way. It had a
Model A Ford motor on a Chevy chassis with a double Buick
transmission and a Dodge rear end. All parts had been recovered
from previous duty, and were recycled in our barn as accumulation suited. Including nuts and bolts, the whole thing cost me
seven dollars, and we used it for all farm work for more than
ten years. It was no honor for a horse to stop and think what
had replaced him. The double Buick power was a strange thing
that always puzzled me—if I put both gears in reverse, the doodle-bug would crawl ahead with invisible speed but incredible
power. Even today, I don't understand how that could be. Now
and then this contrivance would malfunction, but never so often
as the boughten tractors I had later in times of prosperity; it was
the Buckeye mower that usually gave us trouble.

For one thing, the Buckeye mower had some fiber washers in
the gearbox that would endure just about so long and then begin
to howl. We would be mowing away in the sweet grasses of a
bright and lush June morning, bob-o-links a-twitter and wild

strawberries rampant, the world at peace and the breeze properly west, one of us driving the tractor and the other minding the cutter bar, and all at once the serenity would be riven by a yelp that the legendary lost soul with its tail caught in the door never quite came up to. Everybody on the other farms all up the ridge and down the long valley would smile knowingly at the sound of our malfunction. We—everybody with Buckeyes—kept spare washers in the little toolbox attached to the Buckeye, so we'd take things apart there in the field and fit some in. Soon we'd be mowing again, and the pause had one plus—it gave the doodle-bug a chance to cool down. We never called haying off because we had a malfunction.

I recall the time some friends came from the city to endure for a short time the miseries of country life, and we put them up in the west chamber so they could hear the whippoorwills and so the rising sun in the joyous morn wouldn't bound in on them and keep them from sleeping until breakfast, and we said goodnight and retired in friendly fashion. In the morning they came down all droopy and bug-eyed, full of complaints. Hadn't slept a wink. Noises. All kinds of noises. Noises they never heard before. Noises such as a great city never makes. What was this stuff about the quiet countryside? Like for one thing—what was this thing like a motor that kept coming on and going off and went woof-woof-woof?

We never hear it. Every time a cow down in the tie-up sips a drink, the float-valve turns on the pump, and the reciprocating piston does make the house vibrate some. And when the pump shuts off there is a by-pass for the air pressure that goes woof-woof-woof. But we yokels and bumpkins who never got tied into a municipal water system are accustomed to water pumps and never hear them. Did you know that in Japan crickets are used as watchdogs? A cage of crickets chirps merrily until somebody comes by, and when the crickets cease to chirp the silence wakes the householder. You've heard of the lighthouse keeper who slept when his foghorn was blowing, but when it malfunctioned and didn't toot he jumped up from bed and said, "What was that?" If our water pump didn't turn on and off we'd jump from bed and pull on pants and boots and go fix it. It wasn't easy to explain over breakfast that our guests had been kept awake by noises that lulled us. Maybe, too, it would be hard to tell a space shuttler that malfunctions do us a favor—when something isn't working we like to know about it.

Come to think of it, "not working" is the by-word. Much of my planned routine has been interrupted with things like, "Love, the dryer isn't working!" That has been the way the distaff breaks the news about malfunctions. It tells me little, except for the place to start looking. Once, however, I took the washing machine apart and put it back together, and I didn't see anything wrong, so I checked the electric circuit and found the breaker had flipped. I sweat for three days over the thought that I might have sent for a Sears, Roebuck man and paid him $38.00 to reset a breaker. True, I have not kept ahead of advancing technology, and my proficiency in Model T and Buckeye days has not carried over into the sophistication we have now, so that oftentimes the only thing I know how to fix is a breaker. But thanks to space travel, I am again up-to-date, and next time something doesn't work I'll tell Sears, Roebuck I have a malfunction.

6 The Thing Blew Up

In a corner on a stand under the stairs we keep an old-time kerosene lamp—clean, trim, loaded, and ready to go. It is not complimentary to the electric power company, but they deserve that, because we bring the lamp forth and use it during blackouts far more often than we should for the electricity rates we pay. Meantime, there is a fond memory fragrance to that corner of our home, for when we pass we get a thin whiff of kerosene oil which attests the virtues of the good old days. They weren't all that bad! I was fetched up on kerosene lamps, even after electricity. When the rest of our old four-square home was wired the circuit up to my attic chamber was skipped. The rest of the family, downstairs, had light, but when the sun went down my small chamber under the shingles became as dark as it always was, and I had my handlamp to carry up with me when I went to bed. I was well grown when somebody happened to think—why didn't we put a wire up-attic while we were at it? But I was bigger then, and boyhood recollections stay with the kerosene.

The kind of lamp I thus took upstairs in the evening and down again in the morning was said to give the same degree of light as a yellow-eye bean, and I did little reading in bed. I had been well instructed in how to blow it out, and that's why I haw-hawed like a good one just lately when a TV movie showed a Klondike gold miner blowing out his lamp. He was a good one—scraggly of face and a real Service veteran of hunger and cold and the stars. The action was slobby sentimental—he had a flashback to his boyhood by the Keokuk and the sweetheart of his yearning dreams, and now as he finished reading (again) his last letter from her he leaned back in the loneliness of his silent cabin and closed his eyes in reverie. Then he straightened up and brought the day, and the scene, to an end by blowing out his kerosene lamp. He did not turn down the wick according to ancient instructions, but left it high aglow in the chimney as it would have to be for a far-sighted seamstress to thread a needle. Then he sucked wind and typhooned into the top of the chimney. He did not, as I was instructed to do, cup his hand on the far side of the chimney so a gentle puff would suffice. In short, what he did would cause anything except a stage lamp to blow up, remove his whiskers, and enflame the cabin. If that's the

way they blew out lamps in the Klondike, how come anybody survived to pan gold?

In the days of kerosene illumination every kitchen had a lamp shelf, where the illuminati rested during the day. One who carried his lamp to his chamber in the evening was expected to return it in the morning, and midway of the forenoon would come the daily chore of cleaning, trimming, and filling. The parable of Matthew 25:1 and 2 was well understood. A sheet of newspaper was great for cleaning a chimney; the ink acted as some kind of detergent. But if a chimney got sooted it needed washing in a basin in the sink. A home had a special lamp wick scissors for trimming, but it wasn't necessary to use them every day; usually a wipe with a bit of rag would restore the wick sufficiently. Then add kerosene and when the lamp was set on the shelf ready for the next time a nasty-neat housewife would skin a brown paper bag on over the chimney to show *that* chore had been finished. At our house we never used the bits of colored glass that were esteemed by many as a safety precaution.

Magazines like *Home Comfort* carried advertising to terrify people about lamps that blow up. Those advertisements offered packages of colored pebbles for twenty-five cents apiece, postage paid, that were to be placed in the oil wells of lamps to prevent their exploding. Kerosene isn't all that much of an explosive, and in customary use lamps didn't explode. Keep a lamp clean and trimmed, and avoid typhooning it, and problems are few. But the advertising frightened enough housewives so there was a brisk business in colored pebbles and the advertisements ran for years and years. When you sent twenty-five cents and got your colored pebbles, instructions came with it to keep your lamps clean, properly trimmed, and never blow down the chimney, so the pebbles kept your lamp from blowing up and you were delighted. My mother never had any colored pebbles and never had a lamp explode.

I still have the family one-gallon can that brought kerosene oil from the store. I even have the little screw-cap that fitted on the spout—unusual because mostly those screw-caps got lost shortly and a small potato was substituted. Since a can of kerosene without the cap would slosh and sloshing kerosene was incompatible with the groceries in the wagon (remember when grocers delivered?) a potato would get stuck on and nobody ever got butter and sugar that tasted of kerosene. Kerosene, in the days of my little antique can, retailed for seven cents a gallon.

My storekeeping Uncle Ralph once introduced the unbreakable lamp chimney to his customers. Glass lamp chimneys were fragile, as glass goes, and perhaps the constant heat made them so. Sometimes they'd snap for no reason at all. Somebody presaging the age of plastic came up with a non-glass lamp chimney that would take abuse. A salesman called on Uncle Ralph, and he took a lamp chimney from his sample case and bounced it up and down on the floor like an India rubber ball. This kindled Uncle Ralph's desire, and when the salesman threw one against the wall and caught it on the rebound, Uncle Ralph made him a proposition. He said he'd take ten cases, a gross to a case, if the salesman would agree not to sell to another store in Somerset County. Done!

Uncle Ralph had a flair for showmanship, so he contrived a selling gambit. He put all his old glass chimneys in stock under the counter on the floor, and he put his new unbreakable chimneys up on the shelf so he had to climb the rolling ladder to reach them. Then he waited for his first lamp chimney customer. He came in that afternoon—a farmer from Solon who had quite a list, and at last he said, "And, oh, yes—a number 2 lamp chimney."

Uncle Ralph stooped to pick a glass chimney tenderly from under the counter and he set it gently in front of the customer. "Or perhaps," he said, "for ten cents extry you'd like one of my new unbreakable chimneys."

"Unbreakable?"

"Yes—something new, I just got them in."

"Unbreakable?" It was unthinkable!

"That's right—here, let me show you."

Uncle Ralph skittered up the ladder, took a chimney from the box, and let it drop on the counter, where it bounced several times and the customer kept following it with his eyes.

"I'll take a couple."

Before he closed the store that evening Uncle Ralph had sold dozens of his unbreakable lamp chimneys, word of mouth, and he looked forward to a good business. He took the salesman's card from his pocket, looked at it, and added it to those tacked to the wall for easy reference. Nonpareil Mfg. Co., 50 Glenn Street, Rochester, N.Y. Samuel Millins, Sales Rep.

The next day Uncle Ralph had to make good on all the unbreakable lamp chimneys he had sold. They bounced just dandy, and they wouldn't break, but the minute you put one on a lamp the heat made the celluliod explode. Uncle Ralph's letter to Samuel Millins, Nonpareil Mfg. Co., Rochester, N.Y., was returned marked, "Unknown at this address."

7 Much Too Involved

My last communication from John Chase told me that the winter's accumulation of snow came up to 10:30 on his sundial. Which suggests it is high time to set down the true story of A. W. Plummer, M.D., and his sundial, something which caused word to run about town that Doc Plummer had flipped his lid and perhaps should be sent to the funny house. As I review the delightful years that I new Doc Plummer, I'm always able to think of something hitherto neglected, which means that while the old gentleman is long gone, he gets recollected frequently in happy context, and that would well satisfy him as a top-notch memorial. He was GP in our small town, but his interests and scholarship ran far beyond his profession. A real *civis mundis*, he was spare, lean, distingué with a small goatee, and living proof that true gentlemen never specialize. He was "rounded." He could expound on the technique of Praxiteles or defend the philosophies of Rousseau with equal zeal, or turn to show you how to graft a plum tree. In town meeting he would debate a sewer appropriation so it sounded like Cicero in the Forum, and he was a Henry George "single-taxer" Democrat. At church suppers, which he attended faithfully, he would suggest a topic for table conversation, and when he found out which opinion prevailed he would take the other. As a physician, he had completed the required three years at the Maine Medical College and put up his shingle in his home town immediately— there were no residencies in those times—and he practiced successfully and was dearly loved into his late nineties, when he died unexpectedly and caused several patients the trouble of finding another physician. He was in his nineties and had been to attend a patient at Webster Corner when he bounded into my kitchen on his way home to say, "John! There's no place any more to sit and talk!"

I poured him a cup of coffee and got a doughnut, and I said, "You're welcome to that rocker when you please."

"I don't mean that. All the places in town where people sat and talked are gone."

And it was so. Times had changed. The post office, where people congregated to wait for the mail to be "put up," had gone to home delivery, and the settees that served the lobby had been removed. The groceries had gone to chain stores, and managers had no interest in cheeses and crackers and the discussions that went with them. The pot-belly stove was gone—even in the railroad depot, where it lasted the longest. Trains had stopped hauling passengers anyway, and the electric trolley lines had been abandoned. No more waiting rooms. Even the drug store had redone everything, so the soda fountain was a snack counter, the show-globes were gone, and the place was uncomfortable for lingering and talking. The village schoolhouse, which used to have a settee out front that was good for fair-weather lounging, was now consolidated and gone, and the garage now there displayed antiques where the settee had been. The Doc was right; the town had gone out of the sitting-and-talking business. A few days thereafter, Doc went to Ed Prosser, who taught manual training, and told him to have the boys build him a park bench ". . . and send me the bill." The boys did, and for some years the bench was kept in front of the fire station where, occasionally, Doc would sit on it and hope somebody would come by to talk. Times had changed, and we no longer had many talkers. Fact is, Doc didn't last too many years after that. The bench is long gone and long forgotten.

It turned out that Dr. Plummer had developed an interest in sundials some years before he began talking about them. Then he began, and he told us there have been many kinds of them over the centuries—vertical and horizontal, then equinoctial, polar, declining, and so on. Designing one for a particular spot, he explained, calls for careful calculations. You don't just set one up. We could see the Doc had researched sundials with the same interest and care he took with any other topic that came to hand. He was amused when some would ask why he just didn't go and buy a good watch, and some of his friends began greeting him with, "What time is it, Doc?" But after he'd studied the subject of sundials fore and aft, he had Jim Newton, the tin knocker, make him a sundial face from brass, and he was most insistent that Jim follow instructions exactly. Jim said he couldda made the damn thing in fifteen minutes if Doc hadn't been a nuisance standing around telling him how. But Doc was the one to be pleased, and he said Jim did well and the face had all the lines for hours, halves, and quarters set off just the way he wanted them. The next thing was a base, and Doc had Charlie Coombs come and help him mix mortar. They laid up the foundation for the sundial—at the edge of the garden in full sunlight.

For a few days after that Dr. Plummer discoursed on masonry, telling how the Parthenon at Athens had been laid up without mortar, the stones having been cut so precisely in the quarry that they never budged from their correct places. He spoke again about the pyramids of the pharaohs, and also the bricks of bondage which were made without straw and how they must have been difficult to handle. But at the same time, there were enough people in town who hadn't heard the Doc was "into" sundials— enough so the story got started and went around.

Minnie Little mentioned it first. She was coming home from washing dishes after the Grange supper, and was scairt stiff to see a white ghost gallivantin' around on Dr. Plummer's lawn! 'Course, Minnie knew they's no such-a thing as ghosts, so when she caught her breath she looked, and there was ol' Doc Plummer in a Cal Coolidge nightshirt, barefooted he was, and squirtin' a flashlight around like, seem's-if maybe he was picking four-leaf clovers. Or something. Poor ol' Doc! Nutty as a fruit cake. Others saw him like that, and like other ways, and the wagging of heads began. Somebody should do something. Poor old soul could do himself some harm! The selectmen were asked to take steps, and considered what should be done. And, word thus came to Dr. Plummer that he was generating puzzlement and wonder, and pity, and he was tremendously amused.

'The reduction of the universe to a single point," he told me, "requires the values of two celestial bodies in different parts of the sky, and the spherical trigonometry involved is intricate. Then I had to compute true North from the deviation—the inclination—of the needle and the sighting of Polaris. I guess I was too involved to realize a sundial could upset the community."

8 Just Leave It Be

N obody lives in Misery.

It seems a sensitive chap over in West Germany has been living on a street that translates as Scapegoat Lane. It has been Scapegoat Lane since the 14th century, and if the legend has been forgotten we can be sure there was one once upon a time—a legend worthy of the Grimms, at least. But this chap found his finer sensitivities were offended by the name—perhaps he thought people considered him the scapegoat—and he lately petitioned the town council to change the name to Rilke Street. Rilke, we find, was a German poet, which is a dandy thing to know. There is something about this kind of name changing that offends me, so I was delighted to read that the town council denied the request, and Scapegoat Lane continues to be Scapegoat Lane. The town council said if this sort of thing were to allowed, the first thing we knew somebody would want to change the name of Crutches Street. That's a good point.

Back in the 1930s one of our quotable political jokes had to do with the man who came before the judge with a petition to change his name. "Why do you want to change your name?" asked the judge.

"Because everybody laughs at my name. I'm tired of being laughed at."

"Oh? So what is your name?"

"Franklin Delano Stink."

"Ha, ha!" said the judge. "That certainly is laughable. I don't blame you a bit. What do you want to change your name to?"

"Joe Stink."

Which to at least a few people made sense, so we must approach the changing of names with an open mind. But we must also reflect on the humorless nature of a person who lives on Scapegoat Lane and doesn't realize what he's got. It might have been Poet Rilke who wrote, "Nur mit Humor dein Sach bestellt dann lacht dir froh die ganze Weld!" It might have been. That chap on Scapegoat Lane should be told that here in Maine, town of Falmouth, we have the "Underwitted Road," named long ago for some unremembered reason, and that today many respectable and intelligent people live on it without feeling abused. And in all honesty we should tell the chap that "hard-scrabble" seems to have declined. Almost every Maine town had a hardscrabble section—rocky soil, home of the unfortunate. The road out to the hardscrabble section would be the Hardscrabble Road, and the name persisted until the land became residential and farming wasn't important, and people gradually came to dislike the imputation. One long-time Hardscrabble Road is now Bennett Street, which is nothing more than another name for Rilke.

Dry Pond strangely became a victim of this kind of left-handed nicety. Dry Pond used to be in the town of Gray, and it was and is just as wet as any pond anywhere. Nobody remembers what whimsy began that name, but it lasted a long time. Then, maybe fifty years ago, strangers to Gray began moving in and they built lovely summer cottages all around Dry Pond, and missed the point. They took what has to be a humorless poll and decided to change the name of Dry Pond to Crystal Lake.* Maine already had two Crystal Lakes and four Crystal Ponds, as well as a town of Crystal away up-state, but the only dry pond thus ceased to be. Even worse, perhaps, is what happened to No Name Pond. It's in the city of Lewiston, and at one time John Mosho had a cider mill over that way. I used to load bags of apples and a couple of empty barrels, and ride the youngsters over on a Saturday so John could press me some cider. It was fun, and when somebody asked me where I went to get a press, I'd say, "Over to No Name Pond." Almost every time I'd get, "What did you say was the name of the pond?"

No Name Pond isn't that much of a pond, and shouldn't ever get a swank cottage colony that wants to change the name to something that makes sense, but the last time I was up that way I noticed that the road has had a name change. Instead of "No Name Pond Road," the sign now says, "Pond Road." There was once a street in the town of Brunswick named Chickabiddie Lane. It is now Bank Street. But we can be grateful that Moocher's Home, a location in Lower Cupsuptic, is still with us, and so is Boobytown in Dallas. So far nobody has petitioned to change Skunk's Misery.

* Bullhorse Pond, in the town of Industry, was summer-peopled some years ago into Clearwater Lake. Imagine!

Misery, mentioned already, is a wildland township in Somerset County, and so far it has had no residents to contemplate another name. Neither has Misery Gore, an adjacent wildland township—in Maine geography a gore is a triangular bit of land left over after a survey, and sometimes caused by a surveyor's mistake. For name changers Maine's Miseries offer good hunting—there are ten of them in all.

"Slab City" is an interesting holdover in Maine. When somebody moved on and built a water-power sawmill, quick homes were put up for the workmen. The bark side of a log, sawn off before boards can be milled, is a slab, and some of those early houses were nailed up with such slabs, bark-side out, for boarding. Slab City became the name for a sawmill housing area, and even though sawmills of that kind disappeared from Maine long ago, we still have towns with sections called Slab City. Probably that German would like to shift to Shakespeare Corner, or Poe Row. What would that German do with Baileys Mistake? Immortalized forever, Bailey was an old-time ship captain who put into a cove down Lubec way and dropped his anchor in the wrong place. Changing that name to something like Longfellow Reach would be a mistake.

People like that German chap should let well enough alone. Bitte liegenlassen!

9 How Big Is a Fishball?

Marcus Aurelius wrote that when agriculture languishes, a nation is in trouble. And Arthur Lawrence maintained he could tell the condition of the United States by open

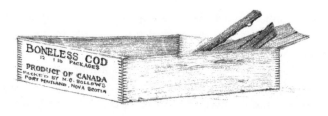

ing a can of fruit cocktail. If the mixture ran heavily to cherries, it meant an overcrop, consequent unloading at short prices, and financial stringency in upper New York state. A shortage of pineapple would indicate Hawaii is in a strong position, selling high. So I am not necessarily odd when I wonder if the erosion of Western Civilization can be foreseen in the decline and gradual disappearance of salt codfish. It has been many years since I've seen a display of nourishing groundfish by the Maine coast—the same coast that once had flakes in every dooryard and acres of them at every harbor, and by catching, cutting, curing, packing, and providing salt fish developed North America and the land of the free and the home of the brave. God Bless the salt cod that made our nation great! But where are the snows of yesteryear, and how long since you looked down upon a beautiful codfish ball on your breakfast plate?

On our hearth we have a handy wooden box just right for a few dry kindlings. It is an antique. I have refused chances to sell it, and many friends have asked to have it when I feel like passing it along. It is of pine, machine milled, with dovetail corners, and there is lettering on each end. In red it says, "12 1-lb packages boneless cod." In blue it reads, "Product of Canada. Packed by N. C. Sollows at Port Maitland, Nova Scotia." It is possible Mr. Sollows still salts a decent cod, but I'm sure he won't be packing it in such a pine box. A box once made by the thousands and available to all packers of fish, and then adaptable to unlimited purposes when the contents had been eaten. A box that could be fitted with a handle to become just right for kindlings—

and for picking berries, going to the store, for keeping horse-shoe nails in the smithy, for Mother's spools of thread, for picnic lunches. A box of a thousand handies, and one that no matter how it's used and for how long will always retain the rugged and nourishing offshore tang of the Blue Nose sea. Except as an antique, the once plentiful salt fish box is long gone.

(Except in memory and in poetry:

> Herring boxes without topses
> Sandals were for Clementine.

And:

> We're the girls from Antigonish,
> We know how to pack the fish.)

Economically, think what that means. It means loss of jobs for choppers, teamsters, sawyers, scalers, handlers, and others who got out lumber for salt fish boxes. Loss of work for the printer, in two colors. No work for the men who made the shook, or the boys who came after school to put the boxes together. All these people out of work, and we haven't come yet to the boat-wrights, the fishermen, the dock workers, and the women who came when the whistle blew with their family heirloom fish-cleaning knives.

Cod was by no means the only fish that got salted. Corned hake was a seasonal delicacy and during the spring runs easy to come by. Alewives and herring had their believers. In Nova Scotia the alewife—L-Y—is a *gaspereau* and smoked *gaspereaux* make good lunch sandwiches; two *gaspereaux* with a slice of cheese between. A Kennebec Turkey is not fowl; freshen a smoked and salted alewife and put the cream sauce to it! The pollock, lesser cousin of the stately cod and the statelier haddock, has a softer flesh and gets marketed as Boston bluefish when fresh—when salted he is said to be "slacked" and he eats pleasantly enough. Here and there pollock still get salted for local and family use—they can be taken up in the harbors and reaches without going to cod and haddock grounds. Get some if you can find some.

Stores used to offer salt fish as "flaked," whole beasties piled up like stovewood, look them over and pick out one you like. One of these would be taken home and hung in the cellarway where it would stay cool. Cut, or yank, off what you want for fishballs or chowder. Split down the middle, glittering with dry salt, such a fish was described by Bill Nye as ". . . lolling about the general store with his vest unbuttoned." Holman Day did a poem about the salt fish dealer in Portland who wrote an address down the salt cod's back, pasted on a sheet of postage stamps, and mailed it to his homesick daughter in Denver. The girl smelled the postman coming and ran to climb his back and bite a hunk, postage stamps and all.

The lore is voluminous. Piety and zeal for freedom, long given credit for colonizing America, had little to do with things—North Atlantic groundfish brought the business, and the first thing the businessmen needed to do with it was put the salt to it. The fish flake, which was a rack for drying split fish, should be the eternal symbol of our rugged beginnings. No home was complete without one, and what's left over was money in the bank. Boats went to England every day. Consider, please, the ancient bit of folk fun:

> An' 'ee comes for'red, ee does, an' ee looks at me, ee does, with tears in 'is eyes as big as fishballs, an' ee says to me, sezzee, "Mr. Finney, sezzee. . . ."

You've got to hunt a long time today before you'll find anybody who knows how big a fishball is. Taxes keep rising, children are on pot and worse, the schools fail us, and if you see a fishing boat today it has been restored by a rich man who sails it in the Marblehead races. This is the story of salt fish, and things are at a pretty pass.

It seems to be a fact.

10 Riches Beyond Wealth

The banks offer generous dividends on invested funds, but that's only money. The big dividend on this spring's fiddlehead hunt was worth so very much more than money—I flushed a woodcock! (Pause: I wish to offend nobody in this great era of abundant offenses—this was a lady woodcock and perhaps I should refer to her respectfully as a woodhen. Maybe a ladywoodbird. Maybe a Ms. Woodbird. Since, at my approach, she lifted off a nest of eggs, I feel she was not a gentlemanwoodbird.)

I have been doubly fortunate. This is the second time in my life I have found a woodcock nest. The first was in my early youth when I was barely big enough to escort the milkers up the pasture lane to close the bars when they were beyond. A shaded pasture lane with tall pines on one hand and some hazelnut bushes and the orchard on the other, a stroll of maybe 500 yards that could take as little as five minutes if nothing happened, and as much as hours if I had the time. The cows were no bother, so whatever the lane offered was mine. The cows, after morning milking, were eager to get on the pasture grass, and capered right along so I had to trot to keep up. In the evening, on the way back to the barn, they knew a dab of grain was waiting in each manger, so they didn't dally. I had a stick—everybody who ever nursemaided milkers had a "soople switch" if a bossy needed encouragement, but it was carried like the baton of a British army

major, and was a symbol of authority rather than a weapon
Sometimes I didn't bother with it. As August came along in one
of my summers I'd begin looking for a Red Astrachan drop—the
Red Astrachan was the first tree in the orchard. One limb reached
over the pasture lane, and if an apple fell on the lane side of the
wall I'd have to fight with the cows for it. By September the Red
Astrachans would be finished and I'd turn my attention to the
Gravenstein about halfway up the hill. So would the cows. Oh—
if I had my stick with me, I'd leave it by the pasture bars, to be
retrieved for the scamper home in the evening.

Our American woodcock is migratory. It is smaller than its
European cousins, the *bécasse* and the *Schnepfe*, but all woodcocks belong to that class of fauna said to have been contrived
by a committee. It's a bobtailed bird in a comical way, seeming
to keep its balance only with much concentration, and it has this
improbably long bill that bends and folds, somehow, and is meant
for reaching into earthworm burrows. We see woodcocks often
enough during a season, and they become easier to spot just
before they take off for the southland; down by Back River they
come out in the twilight for us if we linger after a picnic. During
the day a woodcock usually keeps out of sight unless flushed.
The woodcock is a game bird, with an "open season," but is so
small he might not entice the hunter if he didn't taste so fine on
toast. It takes quite a few woodcocks to justify a slice of bread,
and I suppose in due time our sleepy wildlife commissioner will
add the woodcock to the wholly protected list—as he's done
with the spruce grouse. Finding a woodcock's nest is almost
always happenstance.

That morning, I wondered why the cows hadn't flushed the
bird. They had come pounding along in common purpose, and
were I a bird I'd sooner prefer a small boy's soft moccasin to the
hooraw of a thundering herd. But the cows passed, and the
woodcock rose to my approach, brushing a juniper limb and
whacking a hazelnut bush. My attention thus drawn, I had no
trouble finding the "nest," except that there was no nest. Two

eggs were there on the ground and could have been two feet that way or two feet this way and no never-mind. I kept my distance and admired, and went on to fit in the pasture bars, put my stick in the usual place, and come back again to admire some more. She hadn't yet returned, but the next morning when the cows and I arrived she was there, and she flew up again and now she had three eggs. She made me four eggs in all, with still no nest other than the plain ground, and I didn't think to keep count of the days until the eggs would hatch.

There came an evening when she flew up and let me see that one of the eggs was pipped. The next morning I didn't wait for the cows, but raced up the pasture lane, past the Red Astrachan tree which in woodcock nesting-time had only small green apples, and this time Mother Woodcock didn't rise up. She wasn't there. Nothing was there. During the night the eggs cracked, and with daylight the chicks had been herded off into the bright new world to begin looking for their angleworms. The eggshells had been carried away, and the flat ground betrayed no testimony of a nest. To have seen a woodcock's nest, I realized, was the privilege of few, and of—well, of the privileged!

To see two helps make a full life. This second one was found in the same manner as the first. Older now, and not so jaunty under my packbasket of fiddlehead greens, I was coming uphill from the riverbank, thinking that I would probably rest once more before reaching the road. She burst up, bumping bushes and no doubt thinking to distract me so I'd go away, and there were the four eggs again, on top of the ground and no nest. From five feet I admired, and I turned to call into the trees that I wished her well and I was grateful. I blessed the eggs, then shifted the weight of my basket and walked along. I thought I felt a trifling improvement in my step, as if something had happened to help me. I was wealthy in my lifetime of two woodcock nests.

11 Three Pies and a Cake

The local newspaper continues its faithful favoring of the area without too much reliance on orthography and syntax, and without too much news, either, so that its dominant appeal to the readership is the mistakes offered each time. This time I noticed that Mr. and Mrs. Lewis Orff had a chimney fire at their home in Cushing. The fire department, we are informed, responded and distinguished the fire. After the fire was distinguished a social hour was enjoyed, to which Mrs. Orff contributed two apple pies. We are left to assume that they were hot. It was my whimsy to wonder if the firemen could extinguish one pie from the other, but Neighbor Connie shrugged a Gaelic shrug and told me it was no use. She says she has responded to this newspaper's abecedarian improvisations for a long time, even after postage went up to fifteen cents, but she ceased when the editor printed one of her letters and spelled her name wrong.

The Orff chimney fire, followed by apple pie, is just another in a long list of distinguished Maine fires that are on record if anybody wants to research. In the aggregate fires are statistics and rate as tragedies and disasters, but out in the rural sections they have always had a spectator value even at their worst. This may be merely the consequence of distance—a fire too far from the central hosehouse is mostly a foregone conclusion. It might as well be considered without emotion. Firemen have been known to save only the cellar and the mailbox out by the road, not because of incompetency but because it took too long to arrive. In the small town where I grew up the volunteer firemen customarily stood guard about the village on the night before July 4th, each man with two buckets of water by his feet. They were ready if a skyrocket should find a dry shingle. To forestall major blazes, the chief always tacked a notice to the bulletin board in the post office, calling attention to an imaginary town ordinance:

NOTICE

Under penalty of prosecution, in advance of any fire, blaze, or conflagration, any citizen causing same shall give ten minutes' advance notice to the Chief of Hose Company.

This seemed to work well, but not every small town was foresighted enough to enact such a rule. Too often a building would flare up without warning. Outside of the village, too far from hose and engines, the custom was to save everything that could be lugged from the house and then stand back to see the roof fall into the cellar. There was nothing else to do. More than likely, the firemen would arrive to find the neighbors sitting on the parlor furniture out under the shade trees on the lawn, chewing sandwiches provided by the wimminfolks.

There was one fire in my recollections that was a good deal more distinguished than some others. It was at the Duncan place, out on the Woodchuck Road, far end of town. Abbie Duncan was getting ready to make soap, after a full morning's work in the pantry, so she revved up the kitchen range. It was a Modern Clarion, a larger model with warming ovens and shelves and a hot water reservoir on back. Quite likely the thing got too hot and set off the soot in the chimney. In turn this touched off the roof. Abbie heard the roar in the flue, but she kept her head and cranked the party telephone line in one long, wailing, jingle. The way a crank like that worked, everybody on the line knew something was up, so everybody hurried to listen. So every body

knew all at once that the Duncan place was afire, and the oper-
ator in the village was already in the open window shouting the
alarm to Chief Waterman, who had the barber shop next door.
People arrived almost as soon as Abbie left the telephone, and
in a trice everything in the house had been moved out onto the
lawn to safety.

Everything, that is, except that red-hot kitchen stove. It was
too hot to touch, and Abbie stood there wringing her hands and
lamenting it was goodbye-forever to three pies and a marble cake
in the oven. That's where things stood when the firemen arrived,
their Model T radiator boiling, and shoved a suction hose down
the well. Things looked, just then, like another pitiful country
fire, but news of those pies and that cake put a different light on
the matter. Half the firemen manned the hoseline, and the other
half grabbed grainbags from the barn, for potholders, and they
galloped into that hot kitchen and muckled that Modern Clarion, and then waltzed it outdoors. Took a big risk to do that, but
in the excitement of need things can be done. When Abbie opened

the oven door the pies were just at their peak, and the cake hadn't fallen, as cakes will do if they get abused. Everything just done to perfection for the customary lunch after a fire.

But this time the firemen worked a miracle. They put out the fire. Not really all that much damage—some cleaning up and a few carpenter repairs, and the Duncans would be back in business. Everybody turned to and carried everything back into the house. Everything, that is, except the Modern Clarion cookstove. Nobody could ever figure it out. That stove just would not go back into the house. It had come out, but turn it as they could, and did, the firemen couldn't make it fit to go back in. No way. They'd set it down and look it all over, and measure the doorway again, and they still couldn't get it back. They gave up, and Bill Duncan had to take the stove bolts apart with a wrench and lug the stove back in piece by piece. That was certainly a distinguished fire.

12 Editorial Opinion

Needing to be edified, I eagerly turned the television set to the public channel just in time for the program about grammar, syntax, and linguistic communication as scheduled. There was a fanfare of introduction, and an elaborate technical burst of hooraw for the performing expert, who then appeared with his scholarship modestly arranged. He bowed and took his place on an erudite stool center-stage. Then he spoke. He said, "Whenever anybody, anywhere, anytime, speaks, they're . . ."

I have been timed by my cheering housewife, and I can get my feet off the hassock, unwind my angularities, cross the living room, and turn off my television set in eight seconds. The night they showed the polar bears on the Churchill dump (I have been to Churchill) I made it in seven seconds, but I broke off the knob. Just before I had tuned in, and then turned out, that program of which I speak so slurringly, I had discarded a newspaper because it said certain vaguarities should give us needed incite, so all in all my postprandial and precouchement hour did little for my spirit yearning for cultural improvement. I was fitful until I retired, and dreamed all night in the passive periphrastic.

I've never made a cent at it, but one of my constructive pleasures, almost a passion, has been to mark quick glances. This goes back to a teacher I loved and still love after sixty years who was paid $800 per annum but got $100 extra for coaching the speaking contests and earned her living by doing dressmaking at night. She taught Latin, French, English, some history, and played the piano for assemblies. One day she assigned a theme about taking a walk in the woods, so we all wrote themes about taking walks in the woods. Mine was the first writing I ever had published, because she gave it to the school paper. It was about a blind man who is walking in the woods when a pa'tridge flushes up from under his feet. This would be much like stepping on a bomb. So after the teacher read all the themes about walking in the woods she began the next class with, "I'm proud of you! I have made progress! My teaching career has not been in vain! Out of this assignment I got only three quick glances!"

She said up until now she always got at least ten. A glance is a quick look, so whenever I encounter a quick quick look it leaps at me like the Pacific at Stout Cortez and I think fondly of that dear teacher who taught me so much when I was small and needed it. When I find a quick glance, I reach for a pencil and circle it on the page and hope somebody, somewhere, sometime, will pay attention. I had a certain just reward and a proud moment back along when a townsman and fellow library visitor confided that there's some kind of a nut hereabouts who goes through books and circles quick glances.

I also work, but without effect, on you-knows. Long ago I

proposed a fine of $100 on every baseball player who spits while he's on TV, but later realized the you-knows would pay better. We could fund the national debt in a month if every ball player who says "you-know" were tagged for $100. In one dug-out interview a Red Sox pitcher and the announcer combined for thirty-eight you-knows, and in one sentence the ball player said "you-know" three times. I say "sentence" for lack of a better word for a disjointed incoherence with three you-knows about a pop to short. The infield fly rule was called, you know.

Our local paper recently had its story about a "resignment" party given a teacher who retired. It seems some time back there had been concern about the weaknesses amongst freshmen when they arrived at high school, so a special language arts class had been set up to teach incoming freshmen what the teachers hired to teach them had not been teaching. For eighteen years this retiring schoolmarm had been handling this language arts business with great success, and nothing whatever had been done about getting the other teachers to teach what she was teaching because they didn't. She was so good at it that now her resignment was deplored. She would be missed. I took it the term "language arts" covers the I-could-or-would-or-should basics that when lacking bring on the quick glances, irrelevant antecedents, hung participles, you-knows, and split infinitives. I have always maintained that to, openly and wantonly, with forethought and intent, it takes a good deal more effort than not, split an infinitive. A good English infinitive has every right to properly and proudly, not to say honestly and sincerely, cohere.

Those are my sentiments, and if I'm spared and find the time I plan to extend my labors to give a quick glance at these close scrutinies that our congressmen in Washington keep talking about.

13 That Pause in Worcester

S ome folks stopped by the other day and said they were having a computerized vacation. Before they left their home on the Pacific Coast a travel bureau had set everything up. Even the distance between gasoline stations and the kind of gasoline. Each time they stopped a room was waiting, they had reservations at restaurants, resorts, concerts, clambakes, and when they got to Moody's Diner they knew they would have fried clams and custard pie. They said it was just dandy, all the way. I didn't try to tell these folks about uncomputerized travel in the days of the State of Maine Express, but I did wonder to myself if that fine railroad train might still be running if the Boston & Maine had put it through data processing. The State of Maine Express was an overnight sleeping train from Portland down to New York, and back, and the fondest memory of it can only suggest it was an explanation of why railroads quit.

There'd be a coach or two, but the train was mostly sleepers with a veteran lounge car attended by a steward who had held the Boston *Post* gold-headed cane (as the oldest man in town) for quite a few years. The train made up simultaneously in Union Station in Portland and Grand Central Terminal in New York and passed in the night some place nobody knew where. The pitch was that a Maine businessman could depart Portland about

8:00 P.M. and arrive in New York to do business at 7:00 A.M., refreshed by a comfy sleep on the train. After completing his business, he could catch the same train back to Maine—no hotel bills. There were some flaws in this contention, the major one being the interlude in Worcester. Boston was an oddity in the theory of American railroading, in that you couldn't ride through the city. You could come to Boston from the south and west by the New Haven and the Boston & Albany, arriving at South Station. But if you wanted to come up to Maine you had to find your way across the city to North Station, and then the Boston & Maine would jostle you up to Portland. Nobody will ever know how many confused railroad travelers started from South Station to North Station, or vice versa, and wound up on the Boston Elevated Railway out in Watertown. This fact of transportation was neatly overcome by the Boston & Maine by sending the State of Maine Express to Worcester. This saved, somehow, on "trackage," which is the toll one railroad pays another to use the rails. So, coming down from Portland, the train would leave the tracks toward Boston at Lawrence and go to Worcester. From Worcester the Boston & Maine owned an amusing relic of a line to Providence, Rhode Island, and this connected with the New York, New Haven & Hartford at Providence. It never was, of course, an eleven-hour trip from Portland to New York, so a good part of a traveler's night was spent killing time in the Worcester yards.

Which would be all right if the traveler could sleep, but the Boston & Maine out-did Macbeth in murdering sleep. When the train pulled out of Portland's Union Station, Saco and Biddeford would appear as scheduled, and that was a signal for all experienced passengers to retire to the lounge car and begin getting ready for bed. The venerable attendant tediously provided nightcaps and, if he had lettuce, good chicken sandwiches. This is true; if lettuce hadn't been put in his refrigerator, he couldn't make sandwiches, but offered cookies. The traveler, fortified with a bite and a scotch to lull him, would then go to his berth and brace himself for the night ahead. The train was comfortable enough—the Pullman cars were in good condition and the track to Worcester was well ballasted. At Worcester the locomotive, too heavy for the relic tracks down to Providence, was removed and a yard shifter took charge. The first jerooshling god-awful bump was necessary to get the cars rolling—the shifter just spun its wheels if it tried a straight pull. Back off and strike! In this way the State of Maine Express was run onto a side track to wait until about two o'clock in the morning when the long bypass to Providence would begin. In summer this wasn't too bad, but in winter it meant the locomotive was uncoupled and the sleeping cars had no heat. Gradually, the traveler came to realize the car was cooling off, and then he would feel icicles on the steel by his pillow. Half asleep, as one would be thus, he would wonder if he should go looking for the porter and some more blankets, and then would come another bone-buster of a crunch as a locomotive was again attached.

Do you think I'm making this up? I rode that train many times.

Once the locomotive was in place, the hose lines would be coupled, and presto! the hiss of live steam would be heard—a welcome promise. Then, so soon as to be imminently immediate, the car would be hot as a Methodist Hell and the long-lost porter would appear to open doors at both ends and cool things down. But this was the signal to depart, and now the cars were shifted up and down Worcester, on and off sidings, past the depot and back again, and eventually on the relic railroad that went to Providence. Bumping and shunting and banging, the yard shifter was detached, the proper locomotive hooked on, and the engineer would make several little practice yanks to see if he had been correctly coupled. Railroad buffs of limited experience envy us true veterans who can tell about being yanked out of our pajamas in Worcester. The ride from Worcester to Providence was relatively uneventful, but might be compared to going over Niagara in a barrel. In Providence the preparation to join the New Haven into New York wasn't too different from what had gone on in Worcester, but the passenger could be comforted by thinking how much money the Boston & Maine saved in trackage.

Arriving in New York City, when accomplished, was a well timed matter. After daylight the train rolled along pleasantly on good New Haven iron, and after the spectacular experience of Hell Gate Bridge the passenger, now well aware of electric locomotion, would be ready to step down in Grand Central at 7:00 A.M. and embrace his opportunities. When this was not accomplished, the stately State of Maine Express would fall in behind the commuter trains that somehow proliferated along by Stamford, and then would be sidetracked at the 125th Street Station to wait until all the brokers and stenographers and book publishers and salesgirls had been delivered and it was 9:00 A.M. There is no place in all creation quite like the 125th Street Station to anybody just down from Maine.

Going down from Maine was usually on a half full, or half empty, train. I had this explained to me one time by a railroad man who asked that he remain unidentified. He said they took the berths on the train and divided them up so all the stations above Portland could have some. The sleeping cars started from Portland, but people could come down from up-state by coach. So Brunswick would get so many berths, Augusta so many, and on up the line—Waterville, Pittsfield, Newport, Bangor, even Presque Isle. So when the Brunswick ticket man sold his six berths, he would tell the next customer the train was sold out. Maybe Bangor hadn't sold any, Waterville had sold one, and Portland had sold two. So a train that was "sold out" would set off half empty, and this happened night after night. We had a most interesting man in Maine in those days—Charlie Mallory of South Strong. Charlie was of the hat and steamboat family, and was a broker on Wall Street. He actually "commuted" to his office on Wall Street, going down Tuesday night and coming back Thursday. He told me once, after he'd been doing this for years, that he never knew the "sold out" train to be sold out, and he never bothered to make a reservation. Charlie was on the State of Maine Express so much that he said he could sleep like a baby right through Worcester. He used to wonder how the railroad made any money, and then one day he realized that it didn't.

So when these folks told me they were on a computerized vacation it came to my mind that the old State of Maine Express should have been computerized. That's all it needed.

14 The Judge Smiled

On the 17th of September, 1984, nearly 10,000 people gathered in the Orange Bowl in Miami to be sworn in as citizens of the United States of America. It was the biggest thing of its kind in our history. After United States Magistrate Peter Palermo recited the oath, everybody said, "I do," and then Vice President George Bush made some remarks and said, "This land is now your land!" The cheering was loud and everybody waved the little flag customarily handed each new citizen by somebody from the DAR.

Mike is not his name, but I've got to tell how I coached Mike on American history so he could become a citizen. Mike didn't have the fun of a gang party, but went all alone, sweat standing out, and stood up before the judge after lengthy preparation. Nor did Mike get the publicity of that Miami horde, although he deserved it, and that is why I'm telling about him now. Mike and Mary came to the United States soon after 1918 from what they knew as Hungary but which the League of Nations wrought into Czheckoslovakia, so that here in the States they came to be called Slovaks, a decided ethnic minority in the Yankee town that became home. Mike and Mary didn't know each other back home, but were introduced here by the priest and were married a year or so later. They both worked "in the mill," and they saved carefully until they thought they had enough to buy a farm so they could keep a cow and start a family. Mostly, the folks in town left the Slovaks to themselves. But my grandfather was a farmer, and as he rode past the back yards of the Slovak "mill houses" he noticed that the gardens were lush and fruitful. These Slovaks knew how to grow things! True, Grampie probably was about to fish for the secret of getting so many tomatoes on one vine, but his pleasant hello was taken as a friendly gesture. Mike told the Slovaks that a Yankee had been civil to him! So as Mike and Mary planned to marry, and their savings increased, Mike came to my grandfather one day to ask how he should go about buying a farm. Mary learned English readily, but Mike never did. When he was old, he still had a heavy accent and always shouted in the belief this made his words understandable. Grandfather got the drift, and he told Mike to go to the bank and ask Gimlet-Eye Ferguson to take his mortgage.

Mike did, and hat in hand stood before old Gimlet-Eye, who was the prototype of all the melodrama villains who foreclosed on windows and kicked orphans out into the blizzard. Meantime, Grampie had scouted around and had found exactly the place he thought Mike and Mary would like, and the price sounded about right. Mike walked up the next afternoon and found Grampie hiving a swarm of bees, and he told Grampie that Ferguson had said no. For many years Ferguson had said no to a lot of Slovaks. What would things come to if foreigners like this came to own property in town! Mike didn't seem to resent his treatment, but seemed to feel this was what a Slovak should expect. That's the way things are. Grandfather listened, and Mike helped him put the cover on the new hive, and then Grampie gave Mike a dozen eggs to carry to town for Mary.

The next morning Grampie put Tige in the buggy, and he went

to town and called on Banker Gimlet-Eye. Having thought things over, he was prepared and he didn't speak extemporaneously. He backed Gimlet-Eye up against the wall, poked a finger towards the third button on Gimlet-Eye's vest, and emphasized his opinions in a voice that carried well into the street and assembled a crowd. Years later Lawyer Jack, who had been passing on his way to the post office, said that he never knew the language had so many words to go with "bastard." Grandfather did have a substantial account in the bank, and as an old soldier and president of the Farmer's Union he did have some clout in the community. Mike got his mortgage, he and Mary married, and the rest of his life Grandfather was pleased that he had interceded in such a worthy cause. As long as he lived Mike and Mary would walk over every Sunday afternoon to look in on him, to bring him cakes and cookies, and to report on cattle, crops, and children.

Mary was naturalized before the children came, but Mike kept putting it off and it wasn't until events leading up to World War II made citizenship appeal to him. He went through the preliminaries, and he had to do his homework to be ready for the examination in court. Grandfather was long gone, but I had grown up with the children of Mike and Mary. Once when Mike was laid up I did his spring plowing, and Mary was forever sending over prune doughnuts and walnut horns, and she'd readily give my wife a whole recipe when other Slovak women would hold back a secret. Mike walked in one afternoon with the little booklet from the naturalization people and asked if I would hear his lessons.

I said it would be an honor, but it was also a chore. Mike's language deficiency was not an easy thing to handle. The tutoring took place at random—in our kitchen, in his kitchen, at the woodpile, in the henhouse, under a tree, on the rail of the hayrack, down cellar. He became letter perfect in everything from George Washington's teeth to Calvin Coolidge's milking stool. He labored manfully, but you had to know Mike very well to understand a word he said. I en-nun-see-ate-ted dis-tinct-lee to set him an example, and he tried. There was no question in my mind but that he was ready for the test—at least the minimal test the naturalization people bother with. Mike said no, he'd go alone up to the court house. That morning he had Mary straighten his necktie, and filled with confidence he set forth.

Everything worked out, but Mike was fazed by the judicial atmosphere and the overpowering dignity of His Honor in his robe. When his name was called he stepped forward, sweat upon his brow, and he was alone—he had no cheering Miami thousands to bolster his need. The judge said he would ask a few questions, and Mike nodded.

"What," said the judge, "are the three constitutional divisions of the government of the United States?"

A cinch! Mike and I had gone over that again and again. Time after time he hadn't faltered. Mike gulped. Then he straightened and gained control. His voice, though thick and heavy with his Slovak origins, came steady and serene. Mike said, "The three divisions of the United States government are the President, the Vice President, and the Labor Unions."

The judge smiled. "You may be right," he said. Then he administered the oath, gave Mike his flag, and Mike came home a full-fledged American citizen.

15 The Picnic Pal

I n the interests of household quiet, I have been asked not to shout back at the game shows on TV. The decision to interdict me followed an unscheduled session when I was fetching an armload of wood to take the chill off a snappy fall evening, and somebody had left the set on after "Guiding Light." "Name things you take on a picnic," the quizmaster said, and this was just as I pushed the door open with my foot and came in, not knowing the set was running. With (it turned out) $10,000 at stake, the contestant started with, "My girlfriend."

We had enjoyed one of our picnics that very noontime; not too many minutes earlier I had put away the things we take on a picnic. Even as the contestant spoke. I was running through my picnic inventory, and I had to admit, before I laid down my armload of wood, that it would not have occurred to me to start with the girlfriend. "Quite right!" I called in approval. "The most important thing of all!"

Our picnic, that day, had been a dandy. Late summer, working into early fall, is the best time. Sometimes the tide doesn't cooperate at any season, but today it had been full—we get clamflats at low tide, and although they have their uses, they are not the same as high water. Bright, fallish, blue water reflecting the azure sky, or vice versa, and just the correct persuasion of an Indian-Summer haze to soften the anticipation of rugged days ahead. We (my girlfriend and I) do have winter picnics, too, but that is (and probably will be) another story. So this one today may wind up the off-winter season, and there couldn't have been a better example of salubrity. The frost had been holding off, so we had goodies from the garden—tender ears of Sugarloaf sweetcorn, lucious red Floramerica tomatoes, crisp blanched celery, tantalizing scallions, a fine Straight Eight cucumber, some home-fried Green Mountain potatoes, a snatch of greenbeans, a head of second-planting Great Lakes lettuce, and some other odd items that I shall not trouble to enumerate at this time. Well, carrots and peppers, and a cantaloup. But these were merely to augment and embellish the food, which ran to steamed clams, lobsters brought to fruition in sea water, and a couple of small steaks to take advantage of the glowing embers after the lobsters were ready. I think I have not mentioned the cherry pie.

Our picnic site is a permanent installation. It sits not far from the house, by itself in a sunny dell by the Back River, so the tide is right there when it's high. The fireplace is made of cement blocks, with grill, and table and chairs complete the equipment. The scene is animated variously by sea birds, now and then by a fox who comes by looking for sea birds, and once in a while by a pair of deer that nest just around the bend. On good days a herd of blue herons will disport and cavort, and in early season we are sure of an exhibition of mallards with young. In late season we see immature little blue herons, which are white. Thus my girlfriend and I picnic, and remind ourselves frequently while at it that this world has millions and millions of people who have no idea where we are. This consoles us.

We gain our spot by a sort of roadway through the pines, and I drive my little lawn and garden tractor while she (my girlfriend) rides in the trailer. We could walk, but then we'd have to carry the gear and provender. So I kindle a fire, using good dry wood I filch from my own woodshed, and while I am doing that my girlfriend opens the exercises by spreading a tablecloth. Many picnics manage without the nicety of a tablecloth, but we feel the delicacies of gracious living do no particular harm. Truth is, we have a centerpiece, too—I keep a reformed pickle jar handy and before we dine we pick and arrange some wildflowers. Nicest are the mid-August sea lavenders, a dainty salt-side waif that dries and lasts. But pussy willows, Solomon's seal, blueflag, goldenrod, and fall asters give a refined touch at other times.

So I stood there with my armful of firewood, and I had a warm feeling for this contestant who would take his girlfriend on a picnic, and just then they gave him a big buzzer. "Girlfriend" was not an acceptable answer! So now you understand why I yell back at the TV set and make loud comment about game shows. They (the TV imbeciles) would take beach balls, swimsuits, sun chairs, lotions, portable radios. No girlfriends. So the contestant didn't win the $10,000.

After we (my girlfriend and I) have our picnics we sit as long as we care to sit, and when we get good and ready we pack up and ride back to the house. I douse the fire and arrange things in the trailer, leaving room for my girlfriend. She (who never goes on a picnic with anybody else) assures me she is ready, and I commence the little lawn and garden tractor and thread through the pines for home. I put things away to be ready another time, and she will wash the dishes and launder the tablecloth.

Why would anybody, even TV quizmasters, want to go on a picnic without a girlfriend? No wonder I yell at television.

16 Really Very Nice

I n some states folks have been reluctant to enact a returnable bottle law, but Maine has had one for many years and it does deter highway litter. The beer and pop people did their best to stave the law off, but the voters were smart. Later, the beer and pop people tried to get the law repealed, but the voters were still smart. So I have the occasional fun of going to the redemption center to get my nickels back and I like it. It's good fun. You don't meet friends there, the way you do at the dump and the post office, but you find there can be interesting strangers. Last time I rounded up my summertime accumulation, a matter of $10.85, I got into the place right behind a steward off one of our skin-boats who was unloading the returnables after a week of summercaters at sea.

The fisherman call them skin-boots, because of the sun bathing on deck, but those who own and operate the things prefer the word "windjammer." They are not really windjammers, because they were tall vessels that followed the clipper and the downeaster and lasted into the days of steam. Maine deepwater men went "out east" in windjammers and the manifests would show just about anything you can imagine from teak and tea to guano and gopherwood. These cruise boats that adorn the Maine coastal summer are more likely schooners, which are all right, all the same. So after each weekly voyage of these skin-boats, the steward, or deckhand, will gather up the bottles and cans and hike them to the redemption center to add to his wealth, and he'll come with quite a load. It takes a time to check off his total, and I was right behind one. Behind me, ere long, stood quite a line. Immediately behind me was a tot, supported by his mother, who kept trying to climb my back in his impatience to reach the counter and get his thirty-five cents for his paper bag of bottles. He was a cute little tyke, and he didn't understand why it took so long for that fellow up ahead in the spurious captain's cap to move along. The fellow didn't move along, and he was still handing up bottles, so I made of the little fellow thinking a sweet word might divert his impatience. His mother smiled at me but didn't say anything, and I turned back to wait. When at last the windjammer steward got his money and turned to go, I said to the lad's mother, "Please," and I made a gesture for her to pass ahead of me. Some of this was manly courtesy on my part, because I am like that, but some of it was also to keep her eager son from climbing over me with his bag of bottles.

"Oh!" says she. "But you were ahead of me!"

"True," I said, "but I believe we should be kind one unto another, and I defer to you and offer you my place."

"Thank you," she sad, and then she adds, "and aren't you nice!"

"Yes," I said. "I am very nice."

Now I tell you. Up to this, the ten or dozen bottle bringers who were now behind us had shown no tendency to let the social amenities intrude on refunds. The bottle law doesn't have any clause that says folks must socialize and take an interest, and we had been lined up there rather much as if we were all enemies. The fellow in the captain's cap hadn't yet tucked his money into his wallet and now he turned to look at me as if to see if I really were nice, and he smiled most cordially and appeared to believe I were. "Thanks for waiting," he said, and he aimed this at the whole line.

Behind me and the little fellow and his mother the tension in the line eased off, and a couple of folks said, "Sallright," and "Not at all!" We were no longer strangers together, but potential good friends who had been brought into harmony by a funny. I mused that everybody thought I was nice. The mother boosted the little fellow up onto the counter with his bag, and when the cashier gave him his thirty-five cents she asked, "Now, young man, what are you going to do with all this money?" Everybody was listening for his answer, but his mother said, "Piggy bank! He's a miser; money mad! Every cent he gets goes in his bank. He'll be a lemon and lime millionaire before he's in school!" He had his thirty-five cents clutched in his fist as his mother started to lead him away by the hand. She turned by the door and looked back, smiling. I know we all had the feeling we knew her well. "Bye, now!" she said.

The cashier said, "Bye! And have a good day!"

The man on the back end of the line made as good an answer to that threadbare remark as I've ever heard. He said, "We just did."

The cashier ticked off my total, after heaving out a couple of Canadians cans I didn't know I had, and I got $10.85. About the usual, as I don't go too often. She was affable as hot apple pie, and I'd never seen her smile before. Then she said toodle-oo, and began to banter with the next in line. It was great for me to realize I had wrought some amusement in an unlikely place. Instead of coming home by the numbered highway, I took the back winding road that follows the coves and passes the summer places. It makes a pleasant ride, and just before I got to Maplejuice Cove I saw a shine in the roadside grass. It was a root beer can, tossed by somebody who spurns our bottle law, and the next time I go to the redemption center I'll get five cents for it. The bottle law is a fine idea, and I approve of it.

And I really am nice.

17 All in the Dark

It happens now and then that somebody comes up from a big city to look around with a sneer, and the line goes, "What in the world do you do here . . ." as if nothing ever happens back in the sticks that can hold a candle to the exciting life back there. The parable now unfolding runs like this: Friend Gus Garcelon (this is long before he died too soon) was on the telephone and he said, "How are you fixed to take a week off?"

"Did you have some particular week in the mind?"

"You get the choice one out of fifty-two. How about next week?"

So Gus told me he had invited several friends from the National Rifle Association in Washington to come up to Maine for a week in deer country. "Nice chaps," he said, "but tenderfoots and they've never seen our woods." Gus wanted me to come along and help nursemaid his guests. "Might be fun," I said, and Gus said, "Might be." At that time our commissioner of the Maine Department of Inland Fisheries and Game was Roland T. Cobb, and Gus was a member of his official advisory committee. They were close, and Gus had a blooded bird dog that was named Commissioner Roland T. Cobb. That's a fact; Gus registered the pup with the AKC and he had papers for Commissioner Roland

T. Cobb. One day the real Commissioner Roland T. Cobb had said to Gus that he wondered if it was all that much of an honor to have a dog named for you. Gus said, "How do you think the dog feels about that?" Well, because Gus's guests were from the NRA, Commissioner Roland T. Cobb, himself, extended the courtesy of a warden's camp. The camp was on the Clayton Lake road out of Daaquam, Quebec, and it hadn't been used by a warden for some time, but it was big enough and tight, and it had a woodpile. To get there, we had to drive up the State of Maine, cross into Canada, and reenter Maine at Daaquam, where there were daytime facilities only. There was the Canadian customs station, then a chain across the road at the international boundary, then a United States customs building, next a gatetender's camp for the private chain of the International Paper Company, which owned the road. A short distance from the IP camp, towards Clayton Lake and the Allagash River Valley, was our warden's camp. The border closed at 4:00 P.M., so we got back into Maine in plenty of time and had camp pretty well arranged as the early November evening settled down.

We were the NRA boys, Gus and I, Doc Fisher, Bud Leavitt, and two game wardens—Hank Gauvin who was a district supervisor, and Doc Blanchard who was a biologist. Nine of us. Bright and early the next morning we would hit the puckerbush, and it was our residency task to make sure the three NRA boys each got "his" deer. We had picked our bunks, stowed gear, and unpacked the food. Gus was arranging a big salad, and Hank was stirring the hot biscuit dough. Fisher had the steaks laid out and was fixing onions and mushrooms. I had the stove humping, and the camp was already cozy for comfort and het for supper. The three NRA boys were watching, and were listening in rapt attention to Doc Fisher's well-worn monolog about the time he caught the electric eel in the Islands of Langerhans. He and Gus had a routine where Fisher would make believe he forgot something, and Gus would fill him in. Gus would say, "I think that's right, ain't it, Hank?" and Hank would say, "Eyah, that's right," and Fisher would continue. It was a good place to be, and all at once Hank said, "Dark comes early, gotta light the lamps! *Fiat Lux!*"

Well, we had kerosene lamps, and they were sitting right there on the lamp shelf, but not one of them had any oil. We looked out in the dingle, and found the oil can, but it was empty. That camp had been bone dry of kerosene oil for a long time, and we hadn't brought any on the assumption there'd be some. One of the NRA boys said, "I'll go get some!" and another NRA boy said, "I'll go with you—we'll take my car."

It was already past the edge of night when they left, headlights on, and when they got to the chains and the border they found everything closed and deserted. Leaving the automobile, they hunched under the chains, and walked the rest of the way into Daaquam. The Daaquam store was closed. The sawmill was in darkness. None of the houses responded, and the two NRA boys took their kerosene can to the far end of the short village where a light showed. A Frenchman came to his door, and neither of the NRA boys knew French. All they could do was point to the empty kerosene can and shout, "Kerosene can!"

The Frenchman agreed wholeheartedly, and told them they were exactly right—it was, indeed *un can pour kerosene.*

The two NRA boys returned to camp with the kerosene can still empty, and by that time all was dark and we were making supper with flashlights. Gus held one for me while I turned the camp potatoes. Bud held one for Hank while he fitted his biscuits into a sheet. Doc held one while Fisher turned the steaks. Supper, when ready, was pretty much taken in obscurity, and the company was subdued. We left the pots and dishes for morning attention, and we forewent the customary hunting camp poker game—designed that time for letting the NRA boys pick up the tab for the week. We were all in our bunks by 6:30 P.M., and morning was a long, long time making an appearance.

What about it? Well, that was back in 1965, and that was the very same night the City of New York, and a good part of the adjacency, had its big black-out, when power failed and millions were stranded. We didn't know anything about that big New York black-out until we heard the news the next morning on an automobile radio. Then we realized that far up in the Maine wilderness we had enjoyed a good Manhattan experience.

18 Beevo's Bannock

Having lately apostrophized my boyhood beagle, Beevo, I chanced to pass the pet food display in the grocery store soon after, and I dallied with the brands and kinds. I spent fifteen or twenty minutes there thoroughly amazed at the choices now available for pups and pussies. Beevo would, I thought, likewise be amazed if he could know what he missed by leaving home too soon. In his time pooch provender was unsophisticated and if he got anything more than table scraps from me and windfalls from the neighborhood, it was bannock. Beevo subsisted largely on bannock, and I looked and looked in that grocery store display and it didn't have any bannock at all. I'm wondering what happened to bannock.

Larousse, to which I turn when beginning research into any culinary subject, either for dogs or for people, never heard of bannock, and good *Fannie Farmer* is equally silent on the subject. *The Encyclopedia of European Cooking* says a bannock is made of flour and should be baked in a hot oven for ten to fifteen minutes. This is hogwash and balderdash. My nifty neighbor novelist, Elisabeth Ogilvie, who is just back from viewing the family grouse grounds in Harris with Lewis, says that in the Outer

Hebrides a bannock is always oatmeal and strictly top-of-stove. Oatmeal is absolutely correct for Highland cates and dainties, but in his worst hour Beevo was never subjected to the cruel and abusive bannock of Scotland.

Yet Scotland is the home of oatmeal and bannock. Dedicated dog buffs will, I'm aware, chide me about Beevo's diet, but he got the same thing every meal all his life. He was fed once a day, in the morning, and he was trained never to touch any food that wasn't in his own dish. He had been weaned by the time I got him, but only recently, and it took only a few hours to teach him to bring his dish so he could be fed. "Fetch your dish!" was *bon appétit* to him, and he'd squirm under the stove for it or bring it in from the dooryard. When, in the course of his daily inspection of the environment, he would find a snack at large, he would bring it home for approval, and if I thought it was fit for him I'd put it in his dish. Beevo would sit all a-twitter, head askew and drooling like a fountain, but holding himself obedient until I told him he could eat. Good dog! When we went to the woods to play at hunting rabbits (at which, as foresaid, Beevo was no earthly use) I had to carry his dish in the game pocket of my jacket, else he wouldn't touch his picnic. In the routine of feeding Beevo I came to use four white enamel dishes—I'd take one with food and one with water to the porch where he dined, and bring back the two from yesterday. If Beevo had carried a dish off, he didn't eat until he found it and fetched it. Funny how a dog as stupid as Beevo could be so smart.

In the barn we had a compartment grain bin for the pigs, cows, and hens. It held growing mash and laying mash for the hens, and scratch feed, and then dairy ration for the milkers. The pigs got bran, middlings, and shorts, and then corn meal to hang on the fat. I selected Beevo's fare from that chest. Usually it was a dish of corn meal, and sometimes corn meal alone, but now and then I'd add a handful of this or that from another bin. It didn't matter, because a dog has no sense of taste as we humans do, and he'll eat the same thing over and over. The choice of fancy foods in the supermarket is to please the owners of pets, not the pets. They don't give a hoot. I'd take my dish of grain, however it was composed, to the house just about once a week and make Beevo a bannock, so called.

I think a Scot here and there will support Elisabeth and me in the griddle-cake nature of a true bannock. It was not meant for dogs. Elisabeth tells me the Isle of Lewis bannock starts with two-thirds of a cup of oatmeal, plus a bit more for kneading. Have a couple of tablespoons of melted fat and a cup of warm water. Stir a pinch of bicarbonate of soda and a pinch of salt into the oatmeal and then make a well in the middle. Pour the fat and the water into the well, and stir to a stiff paste. Roll this in the kneading oatmeal and cook on the top of the stove so you have a sort of fritter no more than a half inch thick and about the size of a plate. Cut this in strips with your *sgian dubh*, find somebody to blow a bagpipe, and eat it. 'Tis bonny!

By Beevo's time the bannock and its purpose had changed for the better. I had a discarded kitchen pan still useful, and I'd dump into it my dish of grain from the chest in the barn. When, sometimes, I added a bit of Lay or Bust, the finest laying mash of the day, to Beevo's corn meal I'd smile at the thought of finding him up in a nest. But whatever the grain, I'd stir in bacon fat from the kitchen. We had Liverpool salt for pickles and corning beef, and black molasses to add to cowfeed, in the barn, so I didn't need to raid the pantry for them. For rising, I'd sneak some baking powder, but if I cracked in a couple of eggs I'd cut down on that. We didn't know then that dogs should never get milk, so I'd moisten my bannock with skimmed milk after the cream was lifted for churning and not once did Beevo ever find fault with that. If I caught Mother's kitchen range on the down swing after she'd baked, I could shove Beevo's bannock into the oven, but all by myself up beyond the beehives I had my own outdoor fireplace and a reflector oven. Usually Beevo's bannock was processed up there, and I'd fix myself a snack at the same time. Beevo always helped me.

Sometimes exposure to my campfire brought the bannock to a semi-petrified condition, but we had plenty of skimmed milk for softening purposes. My bannock would last Beevo just about a week, and as the week wore along it took more and more skimmed milk each morning to loosen it.

Which is now all in pleasant memory, and I dredged it up after visiting the pet food display in the market. Not a bannock did I see, and I'm sorry for today's underprivileged dogs. Perhaps Purina and Quaker Oats and National Biscuit will care to take my recipe, above, and put a real dog food back on the shelves. It might not be the right thing for just any dog, but for those with a touch of the good old Beevo—they'd have a money maker. I've left one secret and important ingredient out of my recipe, above, so if they like my idea, they'll have to come to me.

19 CHOO-Choo! (Pang, Pang!)

"**M**ake me a child again just for tonight." I'm not so sure. Christmas is for children, and could I take childhood again for *that* night? The special thirty-seven-page Christmas toy catalog is at hand (batteries not included) and I've studied it in vain for rapport with my glad old days when I and the world were young, and I was a forward-looking Christmas eve recipient. But Christmas is no longer for the Old Boys. There isn't a choo-choo in all thirty-seven pages, and it came to me with a pang-pang that today's youngster won't go for a choo-choo because today's youngster doesn't know what a choo-choo is.

There's talk in high places about keeping Amtrak alive, but out here in the sticks Amtrak means nothing, and daresay there isn't a kid in town ever rode on a train. What freights remain of our old railroads are just putting in their time until the petition to abandon is approved, and trains today don't choo-choo anyway. A toy train meant something back when we could line up by the crossing and watch Mr. Buck turn the cranks and lower the gates for the Halifax Express. That was a train! Mr. Buck would hear the little bell in his shanty that meant the board was green, and he would come out to tell us youngsters to stand back ". . . as the suction could draw ye under!" and we would dutifully stand back as bade, because we all liked Mr. Buck and thought of him rather much as if he owned the railroad. We had seven grade crossings right in the village, and as the Halifax Express hit close to eighty along there the engineer just pulled down the whistle cord and held it down all the way through. Our village was one long howl, and Mr. Buck may have been right about the suction. Then one of us would run to pick up Mr. Buck's newspaper.

Well, the railway post office had to "catch and throw" for our town because the very important Halifax Express didn't stop at little places. The postal clerk would kick a pouch out the door of the car, and then lift a lever that would "catch" another pouch from a yardarm. Sometimes a "green" clerk would miscue, and he'd hit Nichols' barn with the pouch he threw off, and yank the lever too late to catch. But I guess no postal clerk ever missed with Mr. Buck's newspaper. It would whistle out of the car and come to rest anywhere within a hundred yards, and after the train had passed one of us would fetch it for Mr. Buck. It wasn't the same paper too often. The clerks would find a newspaper that had lost its address label, and they would save it for Mr. Buck. It might be from St. Louis, or it might be from Buffalo, New York. It might be in Yiddish or in Chinese, and fairly often it was a Polish-language newspaper from Scranton, Pennsylvania. Mr. Buck always kept a stack of these newspapers in his crossing-tender's shanty, and he always assured everybody that he read them all—every word. But the crack Halifax Express, while it was the queen, wasn't the only train that passed, and those that did deign to come in slowly with the bell ringing and pause at our little station to pick up traveling salesmen and crates of eggs and cans of milk would choo-choo when they started up. There would be the, " 'Board!" and we could see the engineer turn from the cab window to his throttle, and things would churn and chuff and turn and huff, and the stack would choo-choo-choo-choo just the way we did when we got a cast-iron train for Christmas and pushed it across the livingroom floor.

So you can see why I thought with great care when I looked into this special thirty-seven-page catalog of Christmas toy bargains and found a thing called a "voice changer—batteries not included." It changes a tot's voice so he sounds like a robot. Shall we skip, in compassion, all thoughts as to what a robot sounds like when it goes "Choo! Choo!"?

The considerable variety of frivolous toys (batteries not included) in this catalog ignores the old-time belief that gifts should sometimes be useful and "sensible." I resurrect, accordingly, the summer that I noticed what a great many mittens Aunt Lucy was knitting. One day she would be doing some red ones, and when I asked who would get them she drew me aside, looked about for eavesdroppers, and said, "Sister Louise, but it's a secret—don't tell!" Then another day the yarn would be blue, and she'd say, "For Tom, but don't tell!" Everybody, I could see, was going to get new mittens for Christmas—everybody except me. I felt left out all fall, and took on a bit of dislike for Aunt Lucy. But on Christmas morning I got mittens, same as everybody else, and for the first time mine didn't have loops to connect them through my sleeves and over my shoulders—I was big enough now so I shouldn't be losing my mittens. Useful and very sensible.

There are no mittens in this Christmas catalog, either. There is a cash register for pre-school children, which may well be both useful and sensible, but it also attests that the world is still too much with us and late and soon we'll be getting and spending. I presume the cash register will not sell quite as well as the "Secret Wars Tower of Doom." For "only $19.99" (tax and batteries not included) this does include a trapdoor and a chair for ejecting the enemy. It seems to be a companion toy to the "Thunder Tank," which amazingly turns into a mechanical cat with menacing jaw. And there's a "Wheeled Warrior Vehicle" with five interchangeable weapons. I take this opportunity to wish one and all the peace and joy of a safe and happy Yule.

Then I was pleased to find the only toy in the entire thirty-seven pages to which I can relate. An aerial hook-n-ladder for $24.99. Nontoxic red enamel, Ladder rises to thirty-six inches! One of my best boyhood toys was a fire engine, so at least this smidgen has held fast. But mine was a steamer—it was red, too, except for the brass boiler. Bright red, but probably toxic as they came. Three horses; matched, brown. Just like the real one that would roll from the hosehouse when the bell rang—Clang! Clang! Up front was the driver and beside him the man who rang the bell. And the spotty dog. Behind on his platform the boilerman, hanging on. The cannel coal would already be sending up black smoke when the engine got to the street, and by the time the fire was reached steam would be up. The horses were always removed from the traces until the fire was out, and while they were tied at a distance we children could go and make of them and rub their soft noses. They liked that. My little fire engine didn't roar the way fire engines do today—the little steam cylinder just said swish-swish-swish, and that's what I said in the parlor when I was down on the rug playing fireman.

What *does* a robot sound like when it goes choo-choo, or maybe swish-swish?

20 Need a Roof Jack?

Before the hot-stove season I always clean the flue of my congenial shop chauffage, and this time I found I needed to renew my roof jack. So I went up on the roof to fit a new roof jack and pertinent parts, and the job turned out to be a lot more fun than I expected. A roof jack seems not to have made the dictionary yet, even the big dictionary, and it's always pleasant to know something the dictionary doesn't. A roof jack is a device made by a whitesmith to let a fluepipe pass through a roof while excluding the weather. The pipe passes up inside it, and then above the roof the rest of the pipe fits down over it, and all is angled to suit the slop of the roof—which in my architecture is seven inches to the foot. A whitesmith is a tinsmith and hereabouts we call him a tin knocker, and there's no problem once you find a tin knocker. It seems that since the world achieved perfection nobody much is a tin knocker.

I applied to several hardware stores, which can be considered a reasonable way to start. No; they used to keep a tin knocker on the payroll back in the days of hot air furnaces. No; they didn't have any roof jacks in stock. I got all sorts of helpful information such as the tin knocker who lives somewhere up around Somerville but does his work in Newcastle, but nobody could remember his name. Somebody else told me about a fellow by the name of O'Brien, or Gisborn, or something like that, who had just moved onto the Mountain Road, but whether he was a

tin knocker or a radio repairman he couldn't be sure. Then somebody said there's a tin knocker at Garfield Four Corners named Morrison, and when I arrived I found Mr. Morrison knocking tin.

"Mornin'," I said with characteristic affability, "hear tell you can make me a roof jack?"

"Eyah," he said, executing a poignant paradiddle on a pail.

"I need one."

"Right away?"

"You don't have any all made up?"

"Nope."

"Want to make me one?"

"Now?"

"I'll wait."

"Forty-five minutes."

So I came home with my new roof jack. I don't like to rip out old work until I have the new part to fit in, so I was ready. I got two ladders, one with a hook to go over the ridge, and the other eight feet long to reach the eave. I'm no great hand to climb and I'm timid on anything taller than a chair, so I made sure all was dependable. I always hang on with both hands for a while before I reach. I had talked myself into letting go with one hand when I heard a voice from below. "How's the weather up there?"

Stranger to me—he was a fellow from away looking for the Blaisdells and he came in our road by mistake. I don't know any Blaisdells. I told him I didn't know any Blaisdells, and he says, "I see you're fixing your fluepipe." Then he asked, "You got a roof jack?"

"Eyah. I hunted a while, but I found a tin knocker and he made me up one yesterday."

"Too bad," he said. "I got one good as new been in my barn fifteen years—would-da given it to you just to be rid of it."

"Too bad," I said.

After that Pudgy Clark came by. "How's the weather up there?" he called. "Variable wind," I said. Pudgy said, "That new feller over on the Mountain Road's name's Dinsmore. But he ain't a tin knocker—he's a barber."

After Pudgy left I was uninterrupted long enough so I got the old pipes down and was ready to fit the roof jack, and then the foghorn blew. We keep a foghorn by the telephone, and if somebody wants me when I'm not in the house a blast on the foghorn brings me to answer. My wife can make the thing part your hair at a hundred yards. So I most carefully made my descent to get the good ground solid under my laddery feet, and I made it to the house. "Hello," I spoke, "sorry to take so long—I was up on the roof."

"Tha's all right—this here is Morrison. I got your roof jack made!"

"Good boy," I said. "But you made me one already. Tuesday. That's why I was up on the roof."

"Oh, that was you? I didn't know that. Two people stopped by and said you wanted a roof jack, so I made one up."

"That's too bad. But I don't need two!"

"Course not! My goof, all the way. Well, that shows you how things go sometimes! I'll just keep it in stock. Sorry I bothered you!"

My new roof jack, with new fluepipes, was in place well before the hot-stove season settled in. I endured the lingering hours of a rugged Maine winter in good comfort, and meantime—if anybody needs a six-inch roof jack, pitched seven inches to the foot, Morrison has one all made up.

21 Not the Louvre

Culture comes in different sizes, and here in Friendship our village museum is housed in the one-time Cove Deestrick School, a mossy brick edifice of one room that was relegated to innocuous desuetude long ago by New Beliefs. The Friendship Museum does not have the treasures of the Tate or the Louvre, but we do have an enlarged photograph of Wilbur Morse, who built Friendship Sloops. The Tate and the Louvre, of course, do not have an enlarged photograph of Wilbur Morse, so there you are. We specialize in the immediate, and don't put on airs. I recall yielding a franc to join the throngs at the Louvre, but you can get into the Friendship Museum free of charge and probably will have the place to yourself. There's much to see there besides Wilbur Morse.

The numerous Friendshippers who attend the museum as volunteers and welcome the occasional visitor to the treasures were all busy with picnics, ball games, and family reunions, and somebody was needed between one and four. I had never done my stint, so there I was precisely at one to open the front door with its pot-warp latchstring and hang out the little sign that says OPEN. Immediately I had my first visitors. A young man and a young woman in abbreviated clothing swung past on the road, doing their jog, and curious about the museum they loped in to look things over.

A very interesting way to "do" a museum. They didn't really jog past the exhibits, but slowed to a semi-dignified pace, although keeping step and fetching up the knees, and they were thus exposed to our Friendship culture for as much as eight or ten seconds. They came out while I was still holding the little OPEN sign in my hand, and I watched them off down the road, all a-sweat. I placed the little sign on the hook on the door.

Then I went over into the shade of a maple tree, where the museum keeps a picnic table and benches, and I opened my new copy of *Oedipus Tyrannus* to see if there might be some latter-day improvements to the story. Truth to tell, I hadn't looked at Oedipus since college days, and they are distant, but I had seen this new (and different) translation in the store and I felt Sophocles would add a classical flavor to my afternoon at the museum. I looked at the cast of characters and mused that after all these years I still didn't know how to pronounce "Tiresias."

So it was a magnificently crafted summer Sunday afternoon. There was traffic past the museum which didn't stop, and I sat pleasantly and alone under the tree with the ancient tragedy of the King of Thebes. This new translation did prove to be a mite different. The translator explains that it is meant for playing, which made me wonder what Sophocles had on his mind in that same regard, and then the translator says he has used many words which Sophocles did not—perhaps as if Edgar Guest would obligingly rewrite the Psalms of David. But it was agreeable to run through the play again, and I found myself in agreement with Aristotle, for the most part. I've always felt there isn't likely to be much of a future for philosophers who come right out and find fault with Aristotle. I kept ready to close the book and jump up to welcome folks into the museum to see Wilbur Morse, and I figured maybe three hours had passed without an interruption. I went to look at the clock on the automobile dash, and it was ten minutes after one. It was incredible that in ten minutes a messenger had been sent to find Tiresias and had already fetched him back. I was finished with Oedipus at 1:30.

I went to the automobile again, parked on purpose to show the passing throngs that somebody was there, and I tuned the radio to the baseball game. Sophocles was not our only master of tragedy; Seattle beat the Red Sox again. It came to be 3:45 and my stint as custodian of the Friendship museum was coming to an end. At 4:00 I would take down the little sign and lock up. I felt I shouldn't count the joggers, so my attendance count was zip. Too bad to have all that lore of antiquity ready to go and nobody to take advantage. But, I felt, I had done my community service for the day, and I had renewed touch with Sophocles. I had five minutes to go when a station wagon turned in off the road and pulled up beside me so the driver and I were eyeball to eyeball. "Welcome!" I said.

There was a woman beside the driver, a bunch of youngsters in the rear, and at least one dog. The driver was a fine looking man and I thought he had the appearance of a good museum customer. He said, "I was wondering—is there some place down this road where we could stand on a wharf and catch a few mackerel?"

"Plenty of places," I said. "But it's all summer property down that way, and you might get ordered off."

" 'Fraid o' that," he said. "Come all the way from Mass, hoping to get a few mackerel." (Why do people from Massachusetts always say "Mass"?)

"Tell you what," I said. "Skip this road and take the next right and try the town landing. You won't get kicked off, and by the time you get there the tide should be about right."

"Will do," he said. "Gee, thanks a lot!"

I said, "While you're here, wouldn't you like to visit our little town museum and look at the framed enlargement of Wilbur Morse?"

He looked over my shoulder at the mossy brick schoolhouse with the little sign that says OPEN. "No," he said. "I guess not."

22 Never Roll a Biscuit

N o, Mr. McDonald—you don't roll buttermilk biscuits.
Now, isn't this silly? Here are these money-makers who cook and fry and bake and own lunchrooms all over the world, and here am I telling Mr. McDonald that you shouldn't roll buttermilk biscuits.

Well, you shouldn't.

The gentleman has been pushing his delicious hot buttermilk biscuits not only in the television commercials, but on big banners stretched across the front of his restaurants, and millions come to partake. The commercials show a cook with a rolling pin rolling the daylights out of biscuit dough, and it is good to know something that a big man like Mr. McDonald doesn't know. Heave that rolling pin away, kind sir, and never, never, never roll a buttermilk biscuit.

You pat them.

You pat them with love and kindness and more love. It is the rule.

Buttermilk biscuits, you say? The real thing? Aw, come on! For real buttermilk biscuits, you need a cow. Then a boy to turn the crank on the churn. I was the boy, and I know—and then you need a mother to make you turn the crank, and who has muscles enough to spank the butter until it is ready. We churned every Saturday morning—I cranked and Mother spanked. Thus buttermilk is had, and there is no other way. Cultured buttermilk is a delusion, never ripe and never ready, never sufficient unto the day and deed. And except for Thaddy Weems in the story and the McDonald restaurants, buttermilk biscuits were never baked for breakfast. They were intended for Saturday night supper with baked beans, when you also had a fresh churning of butter, and a comb of honey in a soup plate. If we had buttermilk biscuits for breakfast they were warmed from the night before. Pay attention, and some day you may amount to something.

Thaddy Weems, above, always baked a pan of biscuits for breakfast, just for himself. And the story goes that one morning his fire didn't kindle, and he had to thaw the pump, and one thing and another contrived to delay him, and it was already half past six when he shoved the pan of biscuits into the oven. He looked at the clock and said, "Gracious! Half past six already? Where *has* the forenoon gone!" Thaddy made enough biscuits for breakfast to go him for dinner and supper, too.

No. Pat the dough. Have the dough so soft it will sort of drip off the end of a dinner knife; not too dry. I've got to guess Mr. McDonald doesn't have a Rumford Baking Powder biscuit cutter. Makes you wonder. A corn can with a couple of holes punched to defeat a vacuum will cut biscuits all right, but the Rumford cutter couldn't be beat. They gave them away free if you bought the big can of Rumford Baking Powder. Benjamin Thompson, who was Count Rumford, gave some money to Harvard and they set up the Rumford fund, under which some professor thought up a mixture of bicarbonate of soda and an acid to make gas, the idea being a substitute for yeast, and they named the stuff for Count Rumford, who really had nothing to do with it. You can look Count Rumford up—he was quite a rooster. Rumford Baking Powder. Back in the good Rumford Baking Powder days biscuits were baked in wood-burning ranges—and a prudent cook always had a few sticks of dry alder wood to "brown off" the biscuits. Alder isn't a lasting wood, but burns quick and hot, so just as the biscuits got almost-ready the alder wood would be popped into the stove for the finishing touch. You roll a biscuit dough and it won't brown as it should. But you can roll doughnuts all right.

Which brings us to Mr. Duncan. Mr. Duncan lets on that he knows all about doughnuts, ha and ha. Maybe Mr. McDonald would like to hear where this Duncan Donut business really started. It was here in Maine. In the town of Topsham, in a way. Frank Carver was the chief of police in Topsham, and as there wasn't much profit in being chief of police in that town, he had to find other ways to make a penny. One of them was his dance orchestra. Frank played the drums, and he had a piano, a horn, and sometimes a violin. Almost every night of the week Frank's orchestra would play at this hall or that hall, and it really was a good orchestra. It not only played well, but it smelled good. Because Frank also had another business—he friend doughnuts. This occupied his forenoons. The Carvers lived in the brick building on Topsham's main street that used to be the savings bank—it's still there—and he had a room fixed up for doughnuts. Mrs. Carver mixed the doughnut dough, and it was as close to quality as you're likely to get off a production line. She'd roll and cut, and Frank stood by the fat kettles with a stick like an orchestra leader's baton and fry. Drop in the dough, let fry so long on one side, turn with the stick, and when done lift out and set on the drain board. Frank would stand there all morning and fry doughnuts. Carver doughnuts went to stores and restaurants, and customers came to the house, and it was a tidy little business. The Carvers made a good doughnut. But Frank got so imbued with the doughnut fat that he always smelled like a doughnut. When he was playing drums in his orchestra at a dance, couples waltzing past would sniff and get hungry for a doughnut. If you were back to and Frank went by, you'd smell him and know who he was.

So as chief of police Frank would occasionally perform. When he had a case in court he would stand up to be sworn in as a witness, and Judge Joseph H. Rousseau would give him the oath and drool. And one time Frank had to go up to Skowhegan and pick up a prisoner at the jail there, and he got an early start and was in Skowhegan in time for breakfast. He and Judge Merrill of the Somerset County bench went into the Tuttle-Brown Café and were having sausages and pancakes when the run started on doughnuts. Everybody who came in would get a whiff of Frank Carver, and presuming the café had fresh-made dough- nuts as a special would ask for fresh-made doughnuts. Lem Tut- tle-Brown, who owned the place, had never offered anything except machine-cut doughnuts out of a bake-factory downstate, so he had to disappoint everybody and explain that he didn't have any fresh fried doughnuts. But Lem could smell Frank Carver, too, and he was impressed. He could see that if he did have fresh fried doughnuts on his breakfast menu he would be on the avenue to prosperity. He talked to Frank Carver and Frank told him a thing or two, and after that Lem Tuttle-Brown always had fresh fried doughnuts on his breakfast menu and he became known as the Doughnut King. The Tuttle-Brown Café, from that day on, always smelled like Frank Carver. In later years it was said now and then that Duncan Doughnuts got the idea from Lem Tuttle-Brown, but Lem always gave credit to Frank Carver.

23 Our Coat of Arms

E very family should display its coat of arms proudly, and evidently a coat of arms is not hard to come by if you want to put up with the foolishness. Well, a friend of mine who is a lawyer because he flunked out of divinity school came by the other day to borrow some sneakers, and I asked him if an aggrieved citizen has any recourse when he gets caught up in a computer and can't get out. He gave me the following advice: "Ha, ha, ha!" He then told me that he had recently suffered severe anguish and continued emotional distress when, by a computer error, he got twenty-three consecutive monthly bills from the gas company for $00.00. He didn't get excited, but after the third bill he began getting nasty letters impugning his character and reliability, and they became more and more abusive until he was at last brought into the small claims court. There was no great problem beyond harassment and inconvenience because he was able to prove that the bills should have gone to quite another person who chances to have the same name but lives in Yonkers, New York, where there is a gas company. He said that after he convinced the judge he added in a flippant way that he thought he should be awarded punitive damages, and the judge found in his favor for $00.00.

I mention this because our family coat of arms has been in a computer since away back before Christmas, and I have been getting nasty letters. Except that instead of $00.00, I am being hounded for real money. This began innocently enough when my spouse was looking through the junk mail one evening and said, "I didn't know we had a coat of arms!"

"Oh, yes," I said. "It comes down on one side from Attila the Hun, and on the other side it says, 'Made in Taiwan.' "

"It says here," she says, "That I can get our family coat of arms on a crystal goblet. Doesn't say where it's made."

"I didn't know that," I said. "Very interesting!"

"Wonder what our coat of arms looks like?"

"Why don't you buy a crystal goblet and find out?"

"I don't want a crystal goblet."

After a conversational tilt like that, which is fairly common in our family, I find it difficult to turn my thoughts back to some such topic as the reforms in the theocracy of Alcibiades, so I stared at the wall a few minutes to rearrange my systems, and I

wondered what our coat of arms does look like, and why anybody would want it mounted on a crystal goblet. I was truly
relieved when she said, "I think I'll send and get one."

Life has not been the same since.

The goblet arrived and it is beautiful. The coat of arms, even
if spurious, will satisfy anybody. The thing has gules and fesses
and quarters, and a handsome lion rampant on a field of winter
wheat with a knot in his tail, gold, azure, and a motto in Latin,
even:

DEUS MIHI PROVIDEBIT

"What does that say?" she asked.

"It says, *'Deus mihi providebit.'* "

"Stercus," she said, "I mean, what does that *mean?"*

"It's very low Latin," I replied with a sly twinkle of logical
positivism in my roughish eye. "It means, 'Migod but the taxes
are high in Rhode Island.' "

"Very funny," she said.

But whatever it means, we are well fixed for the family coat of
arms as ever were the Plantagenets, and when it comes to royalty we certainly come down from the very first witenagemot.
Since our family forebears came out of midland England in the
company of respectable, if deprived, coopers, thatchers, poach-
ers, shingle shavers, and assorted tax evaders who were asked
to leave by the authorities, this pretense at heraldic escutcheons
is whimsical. If we did have a true coat of arms, it would probably show two pails of hog victuals and the motto "Peace, Poverty, Penurity, and Paucity." My grandfather would have
explained to me in my youth that Peace is a typographical error
for pease, as in pease porridge hot. But thanks to an enterpris-
ing glass blower with a good merchandising specialist, I now
have an armorial bearing which I can put on a bed sheet and
fare forth like Sir Galahad to seek the Holy Grail and rescue fair
maidens in distress.

Having seen what our crest looks like, my wife now terminated the business with the goblet people by mailing a check and filling in the coupon that says quits. Accordingly, we entered upon a long series of month after month when we got two more crystal goblets with the family arms each and every month, and the thing was like that salt machine down in the ocean that keeps grinding and grinding and nobody can stop it. Then I, too, began to get these nasty letters. There was nothing whatever that I could do. There was nobody to talk to. The crystal goblets came from Georgia, the bills came from Montana, and the nasty letters came from New Jersey. I kept refusing all three at the post office.

That was about the time I asked my lawyer friend what I could do and he said, "Ha, ha, ha!" There was a telephone call from a pleasant lady who asked why I wasn't paying my bills, and I begged her to find out why God had forsaken me. She said she'd see what she could do, and eventually she did, but she also said, "You may get three or four more goblets before we can reprogram."

We did.

24 Nothing to Bandy About

It has been demonstrated, I feel, from this and the other that I am not the sort to jump up and down and cheer about the Computer Age, and my only condescension so far is the little dingus on my desk that helps me justify my bank statements and will do square root instantly while I can't do it at all. I haven't even mastered that little dingus, because I can't get accustomed to the way it lops off zeros. I can't figure out what becomes of them. With dollars and cents. Well, four times $1.25 comes to $5.00, but when I put that into my little dingus it brings off just $5, so the two little zeros that represent no-no cents stay somewhere in the incredible innards of the dingus and are gone forever. It should not be so, and I speak from a position of strength. I learned very early, and consequently long ago, that zeros are nothing to bandy about. There was this professor of mathematics. . . .

I admit that when he flunked me it was not altogether his fault, but he was certainly a contributing factor and I owe him more than I can repay. Alone and singlehanded he weaned me from all interest in his subject, and I came out of college serene and pure to take on the problems of the world and amount to something. I shudder to think where I would be today if he had prevailed. True, I can do a few simple things like estimating loose hay in a mow (important once a year at Candlemas) and I can make sense out of the cashier's ribbon at the grocery store. But figuring a transit of Venus is beyond me, and I have always been grateful. I think of that professor often and how much I owe him, and he comes to mind when I fondle the little dingus on my desk, because one of his oddities was the zero. Only one; he had others.

The class I had with him came at 8:30 A.M. on Tuesdays, Thursdays, and Saturdays. Chapel was compulsory then, so we would come from chapel into the classroom by the front door, but he would come from the rear and would be taking his place at his desk just as we arrived. This professor lived in that direction—he came from home through a grove of trees, along a fence, and into the rear door of the building. Now, it happened that a man who lived in the village and worked as a custodian (janitor, then) for the college would park his automobile against that fence in such a way that the professor, coming along, had to step out around it. This was Tuesdays and Thursdays, and on Saturdays the custodian didn't work and his automobile wasn't there. One Saturday morning I noticed that the professor came along, head down as if meditating on Fermat's Last Theorem, his green felt bag of books a-swing, and he stepped out of the path to walk around the parked automobile that wasn't there. I spoke of this to my classmates, so the next Saturday everybody came early to look out the window and watch him do it.

As to the zeros, one morning he gave us a quick quiz. He put two problems on the blackboard and asked us to take our choice and solve one of them. We were to put our answer on a sheet of paper and leave it on his desk on our way out after class. Anything connected with mathematics that gives us a choice has always seemed Tweedledum and Tweedledee to me, so I took the first problem and with the help of my fingers got an answer. The answer was zero. Null; nil; *nichts;* O, *rien;* naught; cypher; nothing; nihil. Interesting, in a way, to occupy your mind thusly and come up with zero.

Having finished that first problem, I wondered about the second, and as there was yet time I figured that one out, too. The answer to the second problem was the same—zero. Also interesting. At the end of the class I put my paper on the professor's desk, and all it had on it was my name and an empty zero. Zero was the right answer, but the professor didn't give me credit because I hadn't indicated which problem I'd taken. I could see, readily enough, that the man was justified in treating me thus, as he had no way of knowing from my answer just which problem I had done. But the matter gave me pause, and upon reflection I concluded I was not by temperament and inclination adjusted to the pursuit of mathematics, and I began to put my attention elsewhere. I can estimate loose hay in a mow all right, and that is something, but I don't step out of my way to go around something that isn't there. And perhaps I've explained why it bothers me when I put $5.00 into the little dingus on my desk and all I get back is $5. You can't tell me oo isn't important. Well, if I'd had a math professor who could tell one o from another . . . I mean—I've been more fortunate than some.

Candlemas day, Candlemas day,
Half your wood and half your hay . . .

If, at Candlemas, you need to know if you have enough hay
to carry your cows over to green grass, you find the number of
cubic feet of loose hay in the mow and divide by 500 to arrive at
tons. (10 × 20 × 30 feet = 6,000, or 12 tons.)

25 Did Byron Like Onion Soup?

W ho was it said, "The more things change, the more they
remain the same"?

Every once in a while I run across a laborious exegesis that
begins in just such a fashion. The thing will start off:

Who was it said, "Alackaday, alackaday, it's rained upon
my field of hay?"

Then it doesn't tell you who it was that said it, and it goes right
along about the Maya civilization, or chess in ancient China, or
whatever the piece is about, and all you can do is read on and
wonder who it was that got his hay wet. That's sloppy journal-
ism, and should be discouraged. It was Alphonse Karr who said
the more things change the more they remain the same, except
that he didn't say it just that way. Karr was born in 1808 and
died in 1890, and he wrote in French because he was a Frenchman. In 1849 a thing of his appeared which was called *Les Guêpes*,
and it included his observation, "Plus ça change, plus c'est la
même chose." A *guêpe* is a wasp, or maybe a hornet, and the

more you look at different wasps, or hornets, the more they seem to be the same old thing. Thus his philosophy is explained, but his facts seem to be in error. The more things change, the different they are.

There was a news story out of the ancient university city of Tübingen, in Baden-Wurttemberg, West Germany, the other day, and while I don't remember what the news was, it made me think how things have changed in that area. I was there on a bright October day in the year 1953, and then again I was there on the exact same day in 1966. I noticed how things had changed. In 1953 I was on one of these missions for our State Department, designed to cheer everybody up, and I had lunch with the staff of the local newspaper. Lunch, in Germany, is not much like lunch in the United States. Here, we say, "Well, let's get together at lunch!" and we mean, "Let's discuss our business while we eat!" The German business man devotes his eating time to eating, and that day a table for that purpose had been reserved at the railroad-station restaurant. Right alongside the tracks, opposite the depot on the Hauptbahnhofplatz, stood an inn a couple of centuries older than the earliest records, and I was told on the way to it that the onion soup was famous. Nobody, they told me, ever ate there without taking the onion soup, and forever the onion soup remained the warmest memory of Tübingen. I would soon see for myself.

I had already been shown all the other wonders of Tübingen, and they are considerable. I'd even been in the dungeons at the university where, in the middle ages, students who were naughty were shoved while they thought things over and reformed. In 1953 the world was having a plague of riots and demonstrations and violence and damn-foolishment that was being blamed mostly on "students." An orphanage would burn down with great suffering, and the newspapers and airwaves would tell us the outrage had been done by students. Students of what? The Tübingen vaults gave an answer—maybe if we stuck the students in a hole somewhere and went off and left them alone for a while they'd come out much improved, and if they never did come out it would be just as well. The students of the middle ages who had been brought to their senses in the dungeons of Tübingen had left their records—graffiti that attested reformation, or something. So now I was to come to the railroad restaurant and experience onion soup.

The traveler who pays attention will find the brown-gravy complexion of any German eating place poses a question—how did the French and the Italians get their undeserved reputation for the *haute cuisine?* You tackle the onion soup in the Tübingen railroad restaurant, and you immediately realize that France and Italy don't know what cooking is. So as we entered upon the considerable challenge of lunch that day, the waiter brought me the guest book to sign. It was something of a book. Leatherbound, it was maybe three inches thick, and at least two feet on the cover. It was a book you didn't hold in your hand, so a place was cleared for it to rest on the table. I leafed through it, names after names, and curious about its beginnings I turned towards the front. Thus I came to the early 1800s, which were just about in the middle of the book, and I found a name I recognized: George Gordon. George Noel Gordon, Lord Byron. The poet. There he was, and over towards the back of the same I was about to add my name. Over towards the back—I could see that the way the years were unwinding the restaurant would need another book within the decade. I did sign my name in that book, and when I came to set down the date I looked up to say, "This is my birthday!" It was.

The host at that luncheon was Will Hanns Hebsacher, Geschäftsführer of the Südwest Presse, and he now excused himself and stepped to a telephone. He came back to the table, and within maybe fifteen minutes a young lady came bursting into the dining room to come up to him in the manner knows as *schnellschnell*. She was flushed and out of breath. She handed Herr Hebsacher a briefcase, a magnificent piece of German-fabricated leather. He thanked her and she withdrew. The host, you see,

97

upon learning this was my birthday, had called his office and told the girl to buy a briefcase and bring it to him. He now gave it to me in ceremonial manner as a souvenir of my visit to Tübingen. I responded and told my only German joke—about the New Deal congressman's wife who met the Norwegian ambassador and said, "Oh, how nice! Our cook is a Swede, too." This always got a good laugh, and it did in Tübingen. So if you go to the files of the Schwäbishes *Tagblatt* and Tübinger *Chronik* and looked up the issues for October 24, 1953, you will see my picture on the front page as a birthday visitor to Tübingen and a great admirer of the onion soup at the railroad restaurant. Not a bad looking fellow. I still have the briefcase Herr Hebsacher gave me, and now and then I use it in the German manner—not for papers, but to carry my lunch.

I did wonder about George Noel Gordon, Lord Byron, about whom I was by no means unaware, and I couldn't remember any references in his poetry to Tübingen and onion soup. When I had a chance to pursue this, I found that Poet Byron wasn't much on food and drink, and I presumed that his exposure to onion soup in Tübingen left him no inspiration. In *Don Juan* he does take a couple of sips of Samian wine, and somewhere he apostrophies the tocsin of the dinner bell. In another place he concedes that much depends on dinner, but little of his verse has any important caloric quality. Indeed, he asks, "What's drinking?" and decided it is a mere pause in thinking. Anybody who goes through life with that notion will never turn out nourishing poetry. There isn't one mention in all of Byron of onion soup.

Then, thirteen years later to the day, I was in Tübingen again, and I took my wife to the same railroad restaurant to experience the onion soup, and after we sat at table I asked the waiter for the guest book. I told him I had taken the onion soup on October 22, 1953, at which he beamed, and that I wanted my wife to see that I had signed along with Lord Byron. He didn't know anything about the book. He brought in the proprietor, and he didn't know about the book. Change of owners, he said. Must have been misplaced. Things changed, he said, and they are never the same again. Except the onion soup. My wife agreed my praise for it was justified.

26 Ted's Unusual Mother

When Jimmie Medloch stopped by the other day it took me a minute to figure out who he was. He's put on a few pounds. I hadn't seen him in years so I was glad he stopped by. "Glad you stopped by," I said. Jimmie said, "I got something I want you to put in the paper." Mostly, as anybody who has anything to do with the papers well knows, people come around to ask you to keep something out, so my interest, and suspicion, became aroused and I told Jimmie to pray begin.

"Because," he said, "nobody ever puts anything in the paper that is sweet and good and kind and pleasant and inspiring and gives the old world a plus mark. You get wars and muggin's and slander suits and plane crashes, and newspapering is a lot like a recipe for blueberry cake that leaves out the blueberries. Nothing ever happens in a newspaper that cheers somebody up and makes him feel good."

Jimmie was the boy in high school quite a few years ago who played a good first base and got a home run on a bunt and four errors, and when I put a piece about that in the paper it cheered up quite a few readers. He played in college, and after college he went to coaching, and for quite a while now he's been the baseball coach at Graniteport High. He's had some good teams, and has brought along a few boys who got a look-at by the big-league scouts. But now Jimmie tells me it hasn't been all peaches and cream at Graniteport High, by a long shot. New-day attitudes all around, and wise-guy kids who need a smash in the mush, and lack of interest and cooperation at home. Same all over, perhaps, and it's just the world turning on its way, but by times it got Jimmie down in the mouth and he'd wonder where we're headed and how long before things bump. So he told me about this thing he'd like to see in the paper, and I quote:

"We always play the last game of the season with the team from down on the island. It's the only off-island game they get to play, and it's a different kind of baseball. They come to the main on the ferry, and they get to eat in a restaurant, and after the game the boys go through the stores before the last ferry takes them back to the island. It makes a crazy game, because it's the only one my team never wants to win. Well, we see these boys having their once-a-year fun, and it just seems a shame to spoil everything by beating them. We don't try to throw the game, but I put in my substitutes and scrubs, and we even let the batboy catch behind the plate. But the island boys haven't won yet. Not that it fazes them. They're having such a good time they just don't care. Happiest game we play and we all look forward to it. Perfect way to wind up the season.

"Well, this year we got a sour note. The island boys began to pack up after the game and one boy couldn't find his cleats. You know—baseball shoes. Spikes. Everybody looked all around, but they were gone, and then one of our boys pipes up, and he says, 'Coach, it may not mean nothing', but I saw Ted Winn heave some cleats into his old man's pick-up.' Now, his name ain't Ted Winn, but we'll call him that if you put this in the paper. Ted's a good boy, mostly, but not all good. He has times. But he's good on second, and anybody who's good on second can't be all bad. But he teeter-totters the edge, and I guess sometimes he gets blamed for things he don't do—anyway, I gave him the benefit of the doubt, and I wondered how to handle things. Could be that he'd liberate some cleats. But I'd told the coach from the island that I'd see what I could do, and I had to do something.

"That evening I went over to Ted's house, and when I knocked out comes a woman I judged to be Ted's mother. I had no reason to think the worse of her, but when she came out I looked her over and I said to myself, 'Eyah, you're one of these modern mothers ought to be paying more attention to what junior's doing!' Out loud I says, 'I was hoping to see Ted.' She says, 'Ted's right inside—I'll call him.' So out comes Ted, and I says, 'I'm hoping to find a pair of cleats that belongs down on the island.' Ted said he didn't know anything about any cleats, and I told him he'd been seen. But he says somebody is telling lies about him, and that's where things stood and I guessed it was time for me to back off.

"But then his mother comes out, standing behind Ted, and she says, all sweet and serene, 'Is something wrong?' 'No, I guess not,' I says.

" 'Something *is* wrong,' she says. 'I can tell—what's wrong? I insist!'

"So I says, 'Ted, want to go inside a minute?' and Ted went inside. I told his mother that I had no proof other than that the kid said he saw Ted heave the cleats in the pick-up, and she says, 'Don't go 'way—you stay right where you are!'

"When she came back she says, 'Ted has the cleats. They're in his father's pick-up truck.' I said, 'Good! And I'm truly sorry. If you let me have them, I'll get them on the ferry in the morning.'

" 'Not by a damn-sight!' she says. 'No way! That's no good! Ted will get up in the morning and go on the ferry, and he'll give the shoes back, and he'll apologize, and when he gets back in the afternoon he'll hunt you up and tell you how things worked out.' "

Jimmie stood there like somebody who has already finished his story, except that there was just a bit more. He said, "So there I was giving Ted's mother one god-awful great hug, and she pushing me away as she should have, and I think all that ought to be in the paper." Before he left, and I haven't seen him since, Jimmie said he planned to work with Ted during the summer and smooth him up at the plate. "He's good enough on second," Jimmie said, "and he's got a good eye, but he swings too late."

27 Startle Your Friends!

The arrival of the seed catalogs divides the year, and I had just finished my seasonal perusal and had mailed in my order. In my youth, this is not the time of year to think about a pumpkin pie—but things have changed. In my youth, by now, the pumpkins that had not been put in pies or fed to the animals would be past using. They don't keep all that well. But now in my creeping age I can cut pumpkins into cubes along in the fall and stick them in plastic bags for the freezer. We can have a pumpkin pie any time at all, and now my cook says, "Bring some pumpkin and I'll make you a pie." She didn't say pumpkin; nobody does. With us, it's poonka, which is the way one of the youngsters handled it, and it stuck. Enough for a pie amounts to just about a pound. That's a plastic bagful. A poonka pie at reasonable frequency perpetuates my cook's popularity and keeps me happy, so my response to this request was unseemly.

"I dreamed a terrible dream last night," I said. "Oh?" she said.

"Yes," I said. "In the first place, it was all in the passive periphrastic, and that's bad enough, but in the second place it was all in full color."

"This is bad?" she said. I said, "Very bad, it comes from the vivid illustrations in the seed catalogs."

"What did you dream about?"

I said, "I'll tell you, but if you don't mind I'll get some rhubarb and a bag of strawberries from the freezer, and you can make me a strawberry-and-rhubarb pie. I don't feel equal to poonka."

Well, this terrible dream shook me up. I dreamed about something like four thousand pumpkin pies that kept chasing me around, and I was in mortal terror. There was no place for the pies, and they were forcing human beings right off the planet. There were demonstrations at the town house, and a delegation of Russians had arrived to beg us to reduce production. She said, "Maybe you better get the rhubarb and strawberries."

So I did, and she went to making a strawberry-and-rhubarb pie, and I showed her one of those seed catalogs. It was on page 7 in that one, but it was on page 54 in another. Giant pumpkins!

Giant pumpkins? What's gone wrong? The proper pumpkin for a pie is the little sugar pumpkin. I never plant them by themselves, but stick the seeds in here and there when I'm planting my sweetcorn. They crawl all around amongst the corn and in that way don't take up any room. But in late years magnitude has fussed up the seedsmen, and every year now they try to sucker us gardeners into giant vegetables. They have green beans three feet long, and sunflowers the size of washtubs, and cucumbers that need support, and now these huge pumpkins. "Startle your friends!" it says. The idea is that you will grow pumpkins so big it will frighten the neighbors. A pitch is made for winning the big blue ribbon at the fair with the largest pumpkin. So it shows a picture of Mr. Howard Dill of some place in Nova Scotia, and it says he crossed some pumpkin seeds and got a hybrid that will grow almost to 500 pounds. He hopes to hit 500 pounds this next season, but last season he got one up to only 493½ pounds—which made him the pumpkin king of all Canada! The seedsmen are now offering this Gargantuan Pepo at five selected seeds to the packet, $2.50 the packet (plus 90 cents for handling). Any gardener can get his picture in the paper with a 500-pound pumpkin. So I had seen a picture of this mammoth pumpkin in the catalog, and there I was lying wide awake in bed staring into the darkness and wondering what this man Dill has done to us, anyway. My dream, which followed, terrified me.

Pumpkin seeds will germinate close to 100 percent. To be on the safe side, let us assume only four of the five seeds in the $2.50 packet will sprout. The kind of pumpkins I grow for pies start from a packet of thirty-five seeds that cost 85 cents, and one packet goes me at least three years. It is from a conservative poise that I contemplate Mr. Dill's achievement. I get four or five pumpkins from each vine, but that is a planned result—I snip the end of a vine when it shows that many blossoms. I could get more. Bear that in mind. But let us, again to be on the safe side, average that off at three. Three sounds reasonable and adequate. Right now we begin to see the threat. From Mr. Dill's four sprouted seeds he will get twelve mature pumpkins weighing 493½ pounds, or more, each, or 5,922 pounds of available pumpkin pie grist. That's very close to three tons!

The quantity of pie pumpkin used for one (1) pie will vary from kitchen to kitchen, and it is my custom to put just about the pound in each plastic bag. But I notice the people who own the "One Pie" trademark put only fifteen ounces in a can. This is acceptable under today's marketing manners—the housewife has long been conditioned to the large, economy size, fourteen-ounce pound box. (The "One Pie" variety is, by the way, a good item if you can't grow your own pumpkins.) So we are looking askance at Mr. Dill as the potential provider of 63,168 pumpkin pies from his small Nova Scotia garden, all by himself. I shuddered in my sleep at thinking about the thousands of gardeners who, beguiled by the pictures on pages 7 and 54, will send in for five wonder seeds and, in turn, produce each his own 63,168 pumpkin pies. On a continuing annual basis.

The next thing to worry about (and I covered this in my dream) is the number of pies consumed by the average family. I would guess that one every two weeks will prove too frequent, but taking that as a minimal average it is easy to figure out that one packet of five seeds would supply a family with pumpkin pies for the next 196 years. In 5 years Mother Earth would be covered with pumpkin pies to a depth of seventeen feet, and mankind would be obliged to eat its way to extinction in order to preserve life at all. Fearsome!

I don't know what we shall do to be saved, but I offer all this as an explanation as to why I'm having strawberry-and-rhubarb pie tonight. And, I seize this opportunity to ask a question of this seedsman in Minnesota. He says, on page 54, that his pumpkin has good tolerance, and "will thrive as far north as Nova Scotia." I just want to ask him which he thinks is farther north—Halifax or Minneapolis?

28 Ubiquity, More or Less

Our other Maine senator got himself interviewed on the TV, and he said that President Reagan, who was fair game at that time, was in "a most unique situation." Nobody wants to be just like anybody else, and I suppose Mr. Reagan was delighted to be thus grammatically elevated into superfluity. We have a journalistic expert who writes about restaurants for our local paper, and she notified us recently that "all restaurants are unique, but some are more unique than others." So things go in a baffling culture where people who use words don't know what they mean. I was in the hobby shop a while back looking for raffia, which I didn't find, and I heard a salesman trying to work off some postage stamps on a customer who doubtless was a stamp collector. "This one," he said, "is in perfect condition—but these two here are even better."

There was an auctioneer once upon a time who was agreeably

astonished to find in the collection of junk he was about to sell a pair of candlesticks which he instantly recognized as valuable. How they came there he didn't know, but a decent commission on them would run to quite a sum, and he meditated on the best way to get the most for them. They were old, crafted by a master silversmith, and intended to sit at opposite ends of a mantlepiece, complementing each other in a genteel and decorous manner. But in his zeal to become rich this auctioneer persuaded himself into a grievous mistake. He decided to sell the two matching candlesticks separately, one at a time, supposing in this way he would get more for two than he would for two together. He was so wrong! When he brought up the first candlestick and offered it as a "unique," his bidders looked at each other amusedly and each had the same thought. "Unique?" Since the candlestick was plainly one of a pair, where was the other? The bidders, wondering, made like Brer Fox and lay low. The auctioneer teased and pleaded, but he couldn't entice a bid.

Then a young man up back who was not a dealer in precious antiques and other junk and who was present out of idle curiosity put two and two together by sheer happenstance and he figured things out. Since one of a pair of candlesticks would be worthless without its mate, why not take a wild and inexpensive fling at a possibility? He called out, "Fifty dollars!"

Ha-Ha! A flurry of hilarity ran through the crowd of experienced antiquers, and they turned to look to see who was silly enough to bid on one candlestick of a pair. The young man handed up his fifty dollars and took his candlestick, to the great disappointment of the scheming auctioneer, and retired to his seat to await Chapter 2.

Chapter 2

Now the auctioneer brings up the second candlestick and asks, "How much am I bid?" At this, the seasoned antiquers who had tittered were dismayed to see the young man sitting serenely on his stool, his unique candlestick in his hand, and a smile on his face which may be described as extensive. Everybody realized that the second candlestick would require coming to terms with this young man, and that the young man knew this as well as anybody else knew it. The auctioneer pleaded, but nobody made a bid until the young man, still smiling, called out, "Fifty dollars!" There was general chagrin, but particularly with the auctioneer, at the sadness of uniquity, and the realization that for $100 the young man had acquired a matched set of Pompeian oxidized silver candlesticks worth $75,000. There are times when being more unique doesn't pay.

In pursuit of this thought, I like to remember that I was never unique enough to be a Rotarian. This is true. I have always had regard for Rotary and noticed that it pleased many people, but it was never for me. I wasn't unique and in those days only the unique could be Rotarians. Membership was limited to one man from each business or profession, and as the editor of the paper that exploited me in those days was a member, no other journalist could belong. This caused me a deep remorse that remained entirely imperceptible. Since the editor wasn't skilled at writing, I had to do the story for our paper about the weekly Rotary Club meeting, and I would go to the hotel and cover the event from the kitchen. I thus had a first view of all the creamed chicken on patty shells that Rotarians consumed, and I never felt deprived and I wrote the Rotary Club stories faithfully and in good spirit. For years the members of Rotary used to compliment my editor on his fine stories.

Then one day I was at my desk writing the speech we would credit to our first selectman when we printed it, being the speech he would give at the dedication of the new Spanish War veterans' home, and I looked up from my typewriter to see a dapper gentleman approach. He introduced himself as a membership representative for Rotary. He explained that until now all Rotarians had been unique, each to his own. But just recently this had been relaxed, and now they had several categories for each pursuit. For example, he said, where formerly only one journalist could qualify, now they recognized editors, reporters, photographers, publishers, and so on. The bars, he said, had been let down and now almost anybody could become a Rotarian. I thanked him for this valuable information and declined, and that is part of the reason I never Rotated. But I have taken some satisfaction over the years at being more unique than some, if less unique than others. Ronald Reagan may appreciate what I mean.

29 Keeping Cool in Maine

I t's hard to beat the old yarns, so why try? One of these self-styled "Maine Yoomorists" rehashed an ancient Holman Day yarn lately, to impress his flatlander audience with the hyperbole of the Maine winter. Holman Day told it well in rhyme. A traveling salesman put up at the Atkinson Tavern on his first trip to Maine, and he left a call for six o'clock in the morning. Had to catch the early train. At four o'clock the proprietor got up, stoked the lobby stove so the dining room would be comfortable, made a good steak-and-potatoes breakfast, and precisely at six o'clock he went up and knocked on the salesman's door.

Having finally got himself warm in the bed after shivering for hours, the salesman now poked his head from under the blankets into a crisp Maine morning, and all at once he decided he was comfortable and there was no reason why he couldn't take a later train.

"Go away! I changed my mind!"

The proprietor, whose name (for the record) was Elkanah B. Atkinson, was proud of the hospitality of his modest inn, and he didn't want any guests going away to say the inn had failed in its public obligations. So he went in and yanked the salesman from his bed, dragged him down to the dining room, and made him eat the breakfast he'd ordered. When it was over, Elkanah told him he could go back to bed now if he wanted to, but that when a guest ordered a six o'clock breakfast at Atkinson Tavern, by the gods he was going to get it. "Some things, we do well," he told the salesman.

I crib this amusing parable from Holman Day merely to show how the yoomorists steal things from Holman Day. If you've heard this next story about the rugged Maine winter before, it's because they stole it from me.

On any pleasant Maine winter day, when the wind simmers down and the thermometer bursts up to zero, there is always wonder about the disintegration of our climate, and the old-timers like to remind of the days when a pot of water boiling on the stove would be frozen solid. Down-playing the rigors of the Maine winter is as old as history. The first chronicler to deal with the verities and oddities of the season was Marc Lescarbot, the scribe of the Champlain expedition of 1604. His style started the whole thing, for he had his whimsy and was by no means a dry historian. He called winter "hoary snow father," probably taking the expression from the Indians who walked on the ice out to the French settlement at Ste. Croix Island to talk about the weather. Lescarbot says the Frenchmen stayed pretty much indoors, and in his diary Samuel Champlain said this wasn't all fun "because the air that comes inside through the cracks is colder than outdoors." They lacked cellars, so everything froze, and the daily ration of cider came by the pond. The first heavy snow-fall came on October 6, right after the last summer frost. By the 15th of the next June the ice was gone and a vessel could bring supplies.

That sounds about right.

After winnowing the tales of tough Maine winters, I conclude in retrospection that my favorite concerns the traveling salesman who, on his first trip into Maine, got off the train in Mattawamkeag on a late January afternoon and sought lodging at the Huston House. Mattawamkeag is a junction for the Maine Central, Bangor & Aroostock, and Canadian Pacific railroads, a place where a salesman covering that forlorn area of Maine would centralize his calls. The Huston House, in turn, catered to the salesmen and had an excellent reputation for good food and good care. The dining room never served a poor meal, and breakfast, dinner, and supper, any day of the week, anything you ordered came with a side dish of baked beans. The landlord now welcomed this new salesman, stowed his sample cases behind the counter, gave him a key to his room, and said the dining room never closes. After a fine supper, the salesman said, "Fine supper! We don't have a place in Barstin can match that!" Then he took his kerosene lamp and went to bed.

It was not only a fair Maine winter night, but it was of the Mattawamkeag persuasion, and the salesman pulled up the quilts and puff after disrobing only to the extent of his shoes and hat. He looked in the closet and found extra blankets, but he just couldn't get warm. It wasn't just the minus-thirty temperature—there was the noise. With each passing moment the ice in the Penobscot River froze more deeply and expanded amongst itself, causing frequent booms which rocked the hotel and jingled the windows. When the salesman at last half-dropped-off, the big CPR night train arrived from Montreal and froze its air brakes during the five-minute pause at the depot. The steam hoses brought out to remedy this made a jerooshly great hissing, and sleep at the Huston House was postponed. The poor salesman couldn't sleep and he couldn't get warm.

So he rose from bed, gathered up all his blankets and quilts, and he went down into the lobby where the big pot-belly stove was glowing red under the persuasion of dry, upland hardwood. He arranged himself in a rocking chair close by, drew his bedding about himself, and comfortable at last soon dropped off to sleep. He didn't even know the landlord came now and then to stoke the stove.

You have to know that in those days prosperity and winter were the same thing. Harvesting lumber was done on snow. This traveling salesman was probably the only person north of Bangor that night who minded the cold. And one of the things that went on in that country was the nightly chore of icing the loghauls. The big steam tractors that pulled sled trains of timber from the stumps to the mill operated best on roads of glare ice. The icing crew would drip water from tank sleds during the night, and everything would be ready when hauling began at dawn. In sprinkling water over miles of loghauls, the crew would get spray, and the water would freeze on their heavy clothing just as it froze on the roadway.

So it happened that Jim Fletcher finished his trick with the icing crew at daybreak that morning, and crusted with ice as a knight of King Arthur would be girded in shining armor, he stepped into the lobby of the Huston House to get a regular Huston House breakfast of ham and eggs and hash-browns (with a side order of baked beans).

When Jim stomped his boots inside the door, the salesman woke up under his blankets by the fire and stuck his head out to see what bumped. There stood Jim, frozen solid.

"Migod, man!" said the salesman. "What room did *you* have?"

30 The Truth About MacHamlet

Altogether too few people realize that I once played in *Hamlet* on the professional stage. This is not unreasonable, because in college I did an in-depth study of the *Hamlet* theme, going back as much as anybody can into the origins of Shake-speare's version—he didn't make the story up, he just improved it. This was the big effort of my senior year as an English major, and I assure you that in my time in college a bit of work was expected. To sum things up, I suppose, the Shakespearean qual-ity was the *thinking* Hamlet—too sicklied o'er with the pale cast of thought. A psychiatric mess, or something like that. Earlier Hamlets, of which there were many, buckled their swashes and rampaged around and weren't much on philosophy. So I do have a fair knowledge of the play, and to be an actor in it rounded out my stage career.

Long after my sole appearance on the stage, as a character in *Hamlet*, I had a merry time at Elsinore. In Denmark, Elsinore is Helsingör, and Hamlet's castle is the Danish royal fortress of Kronberg. To get to the castle one goes along Ophelia Way, and otherwise the city does keep the ancient tragedy in mind. Shakespeare never saw Helsingör, so it's fun to ramble about the castle and go pickie-pickie on details. Well, when Horatio tells the audience the sun is coming up, he says, "But see how the dawn in russet mantle clad walks o'er the dew of yon high eastern hill!" Pshaw! To begin, Denmark doesn't have any high hills, in any direction, and as Horatio stood on the parapet (plat-form) of Kronberg Castle and looked easterly over the sea the only thing he would see is a flat beet field in Sweden. But there are good quotes, even so. On the way to the castle one passes a shipyard with the prows of good-sized steel vessels over the sidewalk, and the post-haste and romage of the play comes to mind—the business that scarce divides the Sunday from the week. And as there are but two beers produced in Denmark, the Tuborg and the Carlson, I had fun with my version of the Great Solilo-quy—"Tuborg oder nicht Tuborg—das is die Frage!"

I had finished college and was doing everybody's work at the weekly Brunswick *Record*, in the early 1930s, when a troupe of Shakespearean actors came to town for a one-night representa-tion of *Hamlet*. Brunswick, with Bowdoin College up on yon low southern hill, was not a complete stranger to culture. The college occasionally invited the public to lectures and such, and stage productions were frequent by the Masque & Gown. But this troupe did not come to town under the auspices of the college—it was the lingering relic of a barnstorming group that had persisted beyond its day and was strictly on its own. Once such traveling companies were numerous, and some of them appeared faithfully each season with new plays. This troupe, doing only Shakespeare, had Portland and Bangor on its schedule, and planned to stop off at Brunswick in passing. The advance man had been into the *Record* office to tell me about this. He gave me a couple of passes, left me poop-sheets on the actors, and took a small advertisement—cash in advance. He affected a Dickens manner, something W. C. Fields would later do much better as Mr. Micawber, and he told me to be sure to put in my story that the company liked to encourage local talent and would use a few Brunswick people as walk-ons. I told him I'd like to try that, and thus was signed up as an actor.

His appearance reminded me of Bill Nye's report of the time a traveling Shakespearean company played *Hamlet* in Laramie, Wyoming. Bill Nye wrote in his review that the entire audience was pleased to see Hamlet die in the end, but everybody was disappointed that Laertes killed him before they had a chance. Nothing like that could be used in the couth and sedate culture of Brunswick, so I smiled to myself and played things straight. I did a squib each week leading up to the big event, and I went to the railroad station to see the actors arrive—thinking, of course, "The actors are come hither, my Lord." I was disappointed that none of them looked like actors. Not like Mr. Micawber, like Sir Henry Irving, like John Barrymore. They were just people. Their manager pointed across the way at the Eagle Hotel and as the actors walked over to it he went in the baggage room to sort out the trunks. This company did ten or twelve Shakespearean plays on tour, but only the *Hamlet* effects would be needed here at Brunswick.

And Brunswick turned out a good audience that evening. One of the English professors suggested to his students that they might profit, so students came with copies of the play to compare, and a good number of the college community joined them. The old Brunswick town hall, since demolished, had an adequate stage with dressing rooms, and the area out front was ample. When I arrived to go in the rear door and join my fellow actors for the play, the front entrance was busy, and I could see that I was drawing a "good house." I went up the stairs (the main auditorium was on the second floor) and was puzzled about halfway up by the skirl of a bagpipe. When I got backstage, I was almost killed by a Highlander brandishing a claymore that could have felled a moose, and several watching him were in kilts. Just how all this came abut has remained an unsolved mystery, but whereas *Hamlet* had been advertised, all the players were ready to do *Macbeth*.

In a way, it didn't matter. Everybody in the troupe did many parts. Hamlet tonight, Othello tomorrow. Desdemona tonight; Portia tomorrow. The First Gravedigger in *Hamlet* would be the Porter in Macbeth, and Caliban in *The Tempest*. But, out front the students had their texts open to the platform scene, so I found the manager and set him right. He passed the word around, and then lit out for the railroad station to get the *Hamlet* trunks.

To allow time for him to return and changes to be made, the players drew the opening scene of *Hamlet*, which has 175 lines, out to forty-five minutes. The scene should take place on the platform in the dark with lanterns, but this time the lanterns were lacking because Marcellus, Bernardo, Francisco, Horatio, and King Hamlet's Ghost were all in Highland tartan wi' braw plaidies an' tiltin' kilts, and e'en their mickle *sgian dubh*. Backstage, the bagpiper was standing in his dressing room in shorts, waiting for the costume that would turn him into Guildenstern.

It was a memorable production. I didn't have any lines to speak except the arrar-arrar-arrara-aw-gaw-gaw that makes a rabble noise. So I mostly stood and watched, and it was truly educational, and somewhat cultural, to see Duncan, King of Scotland, gradually transmogrified into Claudius, King of Denmark.

When I did go onstage, I was one of the three who made up the rabble that broke the door down so Laertes could come in looking for his father. Then, later, I was one of the soldiers who was told to go and shoot—not one of those invited by Malcolm to Scone.

31 Bucket Seats by Prossie

B eautiful full-color, full-page advertising in the magazines tells us that Leonardo da Vinci is helping General Motors with the design of new bucket seats. Good to know this; the last time I spoke to Lennie he seemed satisfied and didn't think he'd make a change. Probably General Motors has made him an attractive offer. Leonardo da Vinci is one of mankind's greats, and it is truly fitting that General Motors should rescue him from undeserved obscurity and find something for him to do. We can all take heart that the poor slob isn't going down in history as the mere doodler of Mona Lisa and The Last Supper, but will be remembered by the upholstery in the new Chevrolet.

Probably all this advertising just means that GM swiped some idea of Lennie's, and really has no plans to put him on the payroll or set up a lavish royalty account in a strong Chicago bank. Corporations have no soul. And no doubt Lennie's almost numberless accomplishments now rest in the public domain. Funny thing about da Vinci is that he didn't follow the advice of Habakkuk (2:21) but left his scholarly and artistic affairs in something of a mess. He made all his notes left-handed, mirror-fashion, upside-down, right-to-left, hindside foremost, and he abbreviated a lot. Nobody knew what he meant until the code was cracked. This explains very well why they had no airplanes, Hoover dams, and things like that back in the 15th century. Everything we know about flying was right there in da Vinci's notes, but all the scholars thought he was describing the meat loaf at the monastery of Santa Maria della Grazie in Milan. Think where the Renaissance would be today if Leonardo da Vinci had used a typewriter!

The news that General Motors has solved the code and found the secret of bucket seats naturally put me in mind of Prosperity (Prossie) Morrison, who lived in the town where I grew up and was our recognized authority on bucket seats, without reference to da Vinci or—for that matter—General Motors. Prossie was lacking in some of his intellectual connections but at the same time had enough going for him so that people pointed at him to prove there's but a thin line between a genius and an idiot. Prossie survived on a perpetual grocery order, which means he was a town charge—a pauper—and what he got at the grocery store was set down and paid for by the town. No frills, just substantial food. The grocers were given their judgment about such things by the overseers of the poor and if Prossie had presumed to ask for marshmallows or guava jelly the grocer waiting on him would say, "By gollies, Prossie—you know, on that I'm just fresh out!" (In those days grocers waited on all their customers, not just poor people.) But Prossie was not the lowest of the low; he was "poor out." This means he lived in his own little house, which was tight and comfortable, but the assessors didn't tax him. People in worse case than Prossie would be lodged at the poor house, or the town farm, and they were listed as "poor in." Prossie kept a pig and some chickens, and had a workbench in his shed where he made odd things—although he was never considered in the same class as da Vinci. That's where he made his bucket seats.

Probably we need a definition. Along the Maine coast, a bucket

goes to sea. There are no pails aboard ship. When a bucket comes ashore, it may or may not turn into a pail. Farmers who tap maple trees in the spring may hang sap pails, and they may hang sap buckets. School children back from the tide, and workmen, may lug a dinner pail, and they may lug a dinner bucket— your choice. The first industry in the New World, back in the beginnings of the colonies, was a sawmill on the Piscataqua River at Pipestave Landing—now in the Berwicks. The magnificent stands of white oak in that area were perfect for the staves and heads of barrels—or pipes. A pipe varied in size, but it averaged at two hogsheads, or 126 gallons. The manner of putting staves together with hoops to "cooper" a barrel was used also for kegs, piggins, firkins, hogsheads, and other containers now found only in antique shops and the dictionary. It is indeed staggering to contemplate the great quantity of such containers made and used as America was exploited—for cod in brine, fish peas, train oil, molasses, and by no means unimportant, the fine New England rum distilled from equally fine Barbados molasses. In Prosperity Morrison's time, all such containers were still much in use.

Prossie began to be a specialist in bucket seats in a modest way. He would take a nail keg or a bucket and fit it with a cushion, which gave him more of a stool than a chair. Then one day he cut part of the staves from a sixty-gallon barrel, so a human form might fit in, and he left the remaining staves full-length for a back rest. He filled the bottom with sweet meadow hay so a pleasant summer-time perfume would linger, and covered it with heavy burlap cut from a feed bag. That completed the seat part, and for the back rest he used a Park & Pollard hen-feed bag, also filled with choice hay. He cut this bag so the Park & Pollard motto was right where anybody would fit his shoulders—LAY OR BUST. But from the beginning, whenever Prossie delivered one of his seats he would collect twenty-five cents. That was his price, small or large, footstool or easy lounger.

After a time, almost every home in town had one of Prossie's seats, but they were for barns and porches rather than living rooms. Tootie Hooker had six barrel seats in his livery stable. Doc Witherell had three on his front porch, and on hot days patients would use them rather than the real chairs in the waiting room. After Prossie became known as a bucket seat manufacturer, a barrel never went to waste in our town. Any spare barrel would be given to Prossie, and usually the giver got it back as a finished seat and gave Prossie a quarter. Storekeepers would give Prossie their empty barrels, and he'd roll them to his house along the street. Apple and sugar barrels were good, and a molasses barrel was dandy, but vinegar barrels were not favored. The acetic acid penetrated the pores of the oak and lingered. Anybody who sat in a bucket seat made from a vinegar barrel would walk away smelling like a pickle. But Prossie love molasses barrels. Not only did they keep a sweet flavor, but Prossie would always get some molasses. Pump as he could, and did, a grocer never quite drained a molasses barrel entirely. When

Prossie was given a molasses barrel he'd roll it home and then put it on sawhorses with the bung down, and he'd always get a jugful. Sometimes more. He kept himself in molasses that way, and when he'd have a surplus gallon he'd take it back to the store and sell it to the grocer for twenty-five cents.

That's pretty much all there is to the story of Prossie Morrison and his bucket seats. Whatever it is Leonardo da Vinci is going to do for General Motors should command something of a price, either in real money or in memory and respect. It's sobering to reflect that GM could get Prossie Morrison for twenty-five cents. When Prossie died the town selectmen had an interesting puzzle to solve. The town owned Prossie's house, so it had to be freshened up and made ready to sell or rent. The selectmen found quite a few bucket seats, a couple of them on his bench unfinished. They didn't find any scientific and artistic notes, such as Leonardo da Vinci left, because Prossie couldn't write. But on the shelf over his workbench they did find a ten-pound firkin full of quarters. Prossie Morrison is probably the only pauper ever to leave an estate. The selectmen gave the money to the Red Cross.

32 About the Rev. Mr. Thysson

Along about the end of January nowadays there isn't much to do except get ready for February, but in the long ago every town could take part in the fun of cutting ice. The electric and gas refrigerators were up ahead and nobody imagined them.

Mr. Bagshot, who had the ice and coal business in our town, paid his help well, and in addition to getting paid for cutting ice everybody was invited to the oyster stew on Valentine's Day. Cutting ice was over when the big rambling icehouse was full, and that took a few days more than a week. The party at the Magnolia Schoolhouse wasn't always on Valentine's Day as such, because there had to be oysters and there ought to be a moon. Oysters came on Thursday, for Friday stews, according to tradition, and moons came according to the calendar. Everybody gathered along about twilight on the right afternoon, and Mr. Bagshot would have his team hitched to a big Nova Scotia rack well bolstered with clean oat straw. Off everybody went to the jingle of the team bells, and Magnolia Schoolhouse would be warm and ready with a copper washboiler of oyster stew on the peak of the pot-belly stove. The school desks had been shoved aside and tables arranged, and after the feed the tables would be taken down so people would dance. Mellie Footer played the fiddle, Teenie Wiggins the piano, and Lester Carter one of his three—mandolin, guitar, banjo.

Cutting ice began when cold weather had made a thickness of about a foot. That dimension would increase as the nights stayed cold, and in an occasional season the cakes got so thick they were difficult to handle. Men and horses on the pond grooved and cut cakes loose, and double-cakes were pushed and pulled along a channel to the runway that lifted them from the pond into the storage house. Pulleys and a cable, with horses, did the lifting, and when the two double-cakes at a time hit the top and began sliding by gravity into the house they gave a fair demonstration of momentum. It was Pooky Kierstead's job to stand at the point of ultimate destination and steer each double-cake into storage position, row by row, tier by tier. He had a short-handled iceman's tool, but more than that, he had the know-how. His was a job where a novice would get killed every ten seconds.

While just about everybody turned out to cut ice, not always for the money but because it was a community need that could use volunteers, the only other person in the crew besides Pooky that had a specialty was the Rev. Waldo Emerson Thysson, pastor of The First Baptist Church. Mr. Thysson was as big through the shoulders as Pooky, and probably could have done Pooky's job, but he came to cut ice because Mr. Bagshot needed good hands and not because of the pay. However, he knew that Mr. Bagshot would keep the parsonage ice chest loaded for free all summer, so he volunteered on a non-profit basis and wouldn't accept a cent. He also knew that a ton of coal would appear now and then in the parsonage cellar without a bill. In this way he was most practical without impugning the clerical nuance he contributed to the scene. I do not mean to intrude misplaced levity here—Mr. Thysson was smart, and didn't bring his churchly manners to the ice pond. He worked as hard as anybody, and while everybody kept things in good taste in his presence he didn't demand that. He was a hail fellow and had good humor. His job was to stand by the channel where the two double-cakes were pushed into position for the steel frame that would respond to the cable and take them up the runway. Across from him was Randy McAllister, and in his good humor the Rev. Mr. Thysson called Randy his Archbishop. In this way the minister kept his spiritual purposes apart, and nothing sacred interrupted the smooth harvest of profane ice.

The place where Mr. Thysson and Randy stood was something of a perilous spot. Every once in a while, in spite of everybody, the steel frame around two double-cakes of ice would slip, and halfway up the runway everything would come loose. The two double-cakes of ice, something close to a half ton, would come back down the runway to point of origin, hellity-bingo! While in theory this was dangerous, in fact it was not—because when the frame jumped loose the cable would go slack, and the teamster would know what had happened and would yell. When a teamster yelled, everybody on the pond knew why, and everybody would yell. Which would alert Mr. Thysson and Randy, and they would run as fast as they could as far as they could before the down-coming cakes struck the water. There would be a jerooshly great BONK and a geyser-like cascade of water such as might crush or drown, and since ample warning had been shouted across the pond, everybody had turned to look. This might happen a dozen times a day, and some days it didn't happen. But when it did there was a hallowed interruption of the harvesting of ice, and everybody paused to ponder on the consequences if Mr. Thysson and his Archbishop had failed to run. It was at this moment, every time, that the Rev. Waldo Emerson Thysson, D.D., would resound all over the place in his deep and resonant pulpit voice in a rousing, "A-h-h-MEN!" This restored the mood, and the harvest would resume.

Usually once, but sometimes twice, Sunday would cause the Rev. Mr. Thysson to absent himself. Cutting ice was urgent, so the work went on, but Mr. Thysson had to preach. On such Sundays, Pooky Kierstead would come down from the icehouse and somebody would take his place while he stood in for Mr. Thysson. It was Pooky's whim to tell people how it was his privilege to "supply" for Mr. Thysson while the parson was away "on other business."

33 Neddie, the Ex-Chief Oiler

When I was reading in the newspaper how the Pentagon will spend thousands of dollars for some slight gimcrack Sears, Roebuck & Company will mail for thirty-five cents, I naturally came to think of something, and this time if was Neddie Philoon and his brief career as a civilian chief oiler for the United States Navy. This was my only exposure to the intricate workings of the Department of Defense. Neddie was a civilian chief oiler for the United States Navy, all right, but he took early retirement as a small protest against wasting taxpayers' money. An oiler, he told me, is a certified expert who goes about oiling things that need oil.

Neddie's background fitted him for his protest. He had been brought up in somewhat stringent circumstances and knew all about waste-not-want-not. He was taught from an early age to use things up, make them do, make them last, and to keep everything seventeen years as it might come in handy. He had to leave school at a tender age and work in a sawmill to help his widowed mother support the family, and every cent he could grab helped hedge ever impending poverty. Neddie had never known anything about prosperity until along in the 1930s Uncle Sam helped himself to a big piece of land in the vicinity and began laying out a huge naval air station. In those days every government dollar was double-measured for the boondoggle value of making work and votes, and the politicians now cheered because so many new jobs would be created in the area. Neddie, as well as many others, took up with the idea, and he applied for a civilian job as an oiler—one of the opportunities being offered to qualified applicants.

I'd known Neddie a good many years, so he gave my name, amongst others, as a reference, and before too long I got a form in the mail for my confidential attention. I said all the nice things I could think of about Neddie, and to make sure I wrote across the top, "If Neddie wants to work for you, you're lucky, and you should hire him as fast as you can." I thought that mightn't hurt too much. After a few days a light-commander from Navy Intelligence came to call on me, and after I quieted down and was able to speak he told me he was doing the interviews about Neddie and did I know of any subversive activity in the Philoon family over the past 250 years. I was going to tell him how Neddie's ancestor was hanged for a pirate in Madagascar, although he did reform and accept Christ just before they let him down, but I thought better of that and didn't. Neddie would have got a smile out of that, but I wasn't sure about the light-commander. Whatever I did say must have been good, because Neddie came over in a few days to thank me and tell me he got the job. He was now designated as an oiler. I didn't see Neddie again for maybe six months.

When I did see him, he was no longer a civilian employee of the navy and he was no longer an oiler. He told me why he had resigned. It seems he went to work, and was duly entered on the payroll and given his ID card and badge with his picture on it, and at that time the navy air station was merely in the layout stage and construction hadn't started. There was nothing to oil. The big runways were being laid out, trees removed, and grading had started, but everything so far was under contract and the navy, itself, was just waiting. Batterboards would soon be put up for dormitories, an officers' club, and other essential buildings, and there was talk that engineers were designing a weather station. But the navy had nothing of its own on the premises. Neddie showed up for work every morning, and two months passed. At first, he didn't mind taking his regular check, but later he did it with a guilty feeling. He was making good money. At the end of three months he was promoted to Chief Oiler and got a rise in pay. He also got three assistant oilers.

This made things some better, because a four-handed cribbage game cheated the time, but even so Neddie was sensitive about getting paid for doing nothing and even with cribbage the inactivity was boring. When the cement slab for the officers' squash court was laid and after it dried, Neddie got his first chance to oil something. The Marine color-sergeant's daughter was roller skating on the new concrete, and Neddie was asked to oil her wheels. But that was all, and Neddie lapsed into another inactive month, aided by his three assistants.

Neddie said by this time the construction was coming along, and one day a crane came and lifted a big hangar into position. Neddie and his assistants watched, and were delighted to see that the huge doors, big enough to take in four-engine patrol planes, were lifted and lowered by electric motors. Neddie got a big thrill from watching the workmen install these motors—the very first items on the whole station that would come under his care. And would give him something to do. Now he could earn his pay. The motors that operated the immense doors were some sixty-five feet above the floor, so Neddie made the official requisition in quintuplicate for an extension ladder, which was promised in two weeks. Next, the place was designated a hard-hat area, so Neddie had to requisition four hard hats. Things were getting busier. Now it would be three weeks. Meantime, because Neddie was civilian help and his going up a ladder would be hazardous, regulations called for the attention and supervision of safety and first-aid personnel, and it would take a few days to schedule this. But at last all paperwork was finished, all arrangements made, the ladder was in place, paramedics were at hand, hard hats were on, and his three assistant oilers were holding the base of the ladder. Neddie mounted and came face-to-face with the first motor—his first chance to oil anything.

Neddie found the motor had sealed bearings—it was lubricated at manufacture and would never need further oiling. He came down, shook hands with everybody, and wrote out his resignation.

34 She Never Screamed

The television news pictures showed striking Chicago school teachers screaming in the streets, and it was not pretty. Makes wonderment. Well, thoughtful folks might wonder why anybody with so little composure and dignity is permitted to tutor our tots. Can't we find ordinary maniacs that won't charge us so much? And, what about that TV cameraman? "All right, folks—now line up here and get ready. And when I give you the signal come charging down toward the camera with your fists in the air, screaming and yelling, and you'll all be on the network tonight!" Rigged TV demonstrations are no longer fooling that many people. Well, there was one solid attribute shared by every schoolmarm who ever waggled the finger of learning at me, and it is an attribute the school teachers of Chicago need to acquire.

Dignity.

I had all kinds of teachers and some were loved less than others, but all of them maintained royal aplomb every moment. That doesn't mean our classrooms were stiff and joyless; we had our fun. Opening the Valentine box was great, our Christmas tree was grand, and even the weekly spelling bee had its moments. But learning was the reason for school, and there was no letting down of dignity. I've been considering some of the things that happened that might cause a teacher to scream her head off. None did.

Calm always prevailed. Does anybody go back to the World War days when the "tank" was new? It was introduced into warfare by the British, before the United States got into that one, and instead of wheels it had all-terrain tracks that "it puts down and picks up again as it goes." The thing was new to war and new to the outside world, but here in Maine it was old stuff— the Lombard factory at Waterville had been making steam log haulers for years. The Lombard steam logging tractor was prototype to both the military tank and the "caterpillar" heavy equipment that came later. Lombard tried to collect when his patented tracks were copied, but litigation dragged on and he never did.

Anyway, knowing all about cleated tractor power, we boys used to make tanks, even before there were tanks, from sewing-thread spools and rubber bands. The rubber band through the hole in the spool, twisted well, was the power, and we cut notches in the rims of the spool to give the effect of the "caterpillar." Our little toys would climb over small things, just as a Lombard would twitch logs in the woods. The appearance of the "tank" in the war news created a new interest, and we stopped making Lombards and began making tanks. Our tanks could fight great battles in the schoolyard, but our teachers forbade any such hostilities inside the building.

Merton Ridley improved on our simple design. Mert's father was a boss in the shoe factory, and Mert was able to come by one of the oversize spools used on the factory stitching machines. A stitcher would put hundreds of pairs of shoes together before one of those spools ran out of thread—they were close to a foot long and had a circumference of 5 or 6 inches. Ordinary rubber bands wouldn't have the strength to drive such a tank, so Merton cut off a section of a 30-×-3½ Model T inner tube, and instead of a wooden match for the push stick he used a ¼-inch dowel. When he got this monster constructed, Merton let it go in the barn, and watched in awe as it roared across the floor, knocked over some paint pails, and assaulted the wall so several garden tools popped off their pegs. The thing churned away against the wall until the inner tube rubber unwound, and it sounded like the stick on a picket fence. Merton realized he had something.

Mrs. Mathewson was an excellent teacher who brooked no dalliance; her word was law, and her dignity was solid. Even as she walked to school, not yet in her throne room, she maintained the stately tread of Mother Juno, and everybody could see that she was in constant command. She was on the stout side, perhaps reminding also of Victoria Regina, and in the classroom she could yank a boy out of his seat by the scruff of his neck and slam him against the wall so the pictures of Washington and Lincoln went askew. She had never been cowed by the biggest, most muscular and athletic, of her pupils, and when she did slam one of them against the wall she did it with the poise, charm, and grace of a figure skater taking a gold at the Olympic Games. She never screamed.

On this occasion, Mrs. Mathewson was at the front blackboard showing how to diagram a sentence, and with her back to the class she was unaware that Merton had taken his monster tank from his desk and was fondling it with complete absorption about its kinetic principle. Mrs. Mathewson was saying that "sweetly" was an adverb to be related to the transitive verb "sing" when Merton lost control and his tank started down the aisle. It sounded much like a team of horses trotting a loaded hayrack across a wooden bridge, and as it approached Mrs. Mathewson was saying, ". . . the direct object being . . ." Then she lifted one foot to let the tank pass and thump the wall and churn itself out. "Merton," she interrupted unruffled, "please take your tank to the principal's office and mention my name." Then she said, ". . . the direct object being the word 'song.' " She did not scream and she was never on the TV.

35 Cappy, and *Blossom*, Retire

Cappy has retired from lobstering, and he sold *Blossom* down the river—well, over to Pleasant Point. A Maine lobster-catcher's boat, when on mooring in the hah-b'h, is a gladsome thing, with her own style and beauty. And she's a worthy craft at work "down below," biting into the swells and bringing her skipper and booty safe home to the mooring. Built for business, a lobster boat has little truck with and no esteem for the summer playthings that insist on being in the way and all too often foul the warps of her traps. But of late years the lobster boat has become similar to "summer mahogany" in one respect—more and more of them get "hauled" for the winter.

Back along, almost all the lobster-fishing boats remained in the water from season to season, and a good many of them worked all winter. If a lobster boat wasn't working, she just lolled there on mooring. She'd get a check-up at intervals—the engine would be started, snow pushed off the washboards, and the bilge pumped if needed. Now and then a skin of ice might form over the harbor, and this could start the caulking in the seams and before going to sea again the boat would get a "chinzing." That's a repair job to close her seams. For a chinzing, the boat gets beached out by the low tide, but not really "hauled."

So *Blossom*, even though Cappy didn't fish in the winter, stayed in the water, and I surmised something was afoot when I heard, one October, that he had hauled *Blossom* and she was in her cradle over by Salt Pond. Just like a yacht. There comes a time. . . . Might be that come spring Cappy would freshen her with new paint and copper, and go again to set traps. Or, which turned out to be the case, he was retiring and *Blossom* was on the market. So I'd been expecting Cappy to stop by soon, and he did. Wearing a new pair of rubber boots, he betrayed that he was now clamming. He could make a pretty penny at that until ice froze on the clam flats, and then he could stay in the kitchen and feed the fire. Clams had been fetching some twenty-eight dollars a hod, so there was no need to worry about Cappy.

"Clammin'?" I said.

"Eyah. Some."

There are deep-seated esoterics to Maine coastal affairs, and a converted highlander of my precocious ignorance will never master them all, but one thing is to speak sparingly and convey much. My question, i.e., "Clammin'?" (when rendered into tidal purposes) would mean, "I heard *Blossom* was hauled, and I see by your boots that you've gone to digging clams."

Cappy confirmed. "Comin?" I asked.

"Not good. Don't seem to be no holes."

Clams, in mud, work like suction pumps, sucking in water that contains sustenance, and then squirting it out after partaking. The squirting makes holes in the mud, and each hole tells where a clam lurks. "Must be there," I said.

"They're they-yer all right, but they ain't working."

"Today's prices," I said, "and you don't need to find too many holes."

"They's diff'ent ways to look at that."

And so on, and while I knew why Cappy was calling, he delayed bringing the subject up and I allowed him to. Before he got around to the subject I tossed a hammer, saw, knife, and some other tools into my carrying box, so I was all ready. We were going to fit a weather cover over *Blossom* to fend off snow and rain. "I got a piece o' plarstick," said Cappy, "twenty by twenty."

"And gopher wood?" I twitted.

Cappy's no stranger to the Noah story, so he said, "Eyah, cubits and cubits."

We went to the scene, and there was lovely *Blossom* perched up in the air with a certain forlorn and misplaced charm. We worked off ladders and it didn't take too long to make a frame with pieces of two-by-twice and some strapping. Then we unfolded the plastic and fitted it to protect *Blossom* from the blizzards and blusters ahead. She was snug, and I suggest to all craftsmen everywhere that they do no bragging until they've fitted a square of plastic, twenty by twenty, over a cradled lobster boat during a whirligig coastal breeze that is making whitecaps in the river. We picked up the litter from our work and took away the ladders, and we stood there to eye our job. *Blossom*, out of water and canopied, looked about the same as any old yacht. Cappy said he wanted to "make it all right with me," and I said I didn't have change for a dollar. He said he didn't mean to put me to no trouble 'thout gettin' even. I said I'd send a bill. He said, "You do that."

Which was riddle-talk, because the way Cappy has always settled his favors with me was to stop by on a pleasant summer afternoon and shore-talk, and sooner or later he'd ask, " 'Bout ha-pas-two?"

"Sounds about right with me."

"I'm settin' traps," Cappy would say.

Going down the bay with Cappy and *Blossom* to see the sun come out of the ocean on a good "haulin' day" is a kind of paycheck not too many people ever earn. Finest kind.

But, that winter Cappy sold *Blossom* and went out of the lobster-fishing business forever. Traps and all. I suppose he owes me, but there won't be any bill.

36 Christmas at Auntie Clara's

Compared to the demand for them, there aren't that many good Christmas stories, so I'll set down the tale of the time Auntie Clara entertained. Auntie Clara was High Church, which made her unusual in our flourishing family of Low Church and then very-Low-Church indeed, as well as strayed Congregationalists, Baptists, and even a few Uni-Uni's. The family naturally handled a High-Churcher much askance, but Auntie Clara was always bidden to Christmas dinner and she always came. Just what she was to us remained obscure—some said she was a button-hole relative and others limited her to a woodpile cousin. She had inherited 400 acres of choice meadowland, a fourteen-room house, and a forty-cow barn from a distant uncle of ours that nobody could remember, and she lived a spinster. She had money. So she kept a man and his wife as "help." On Christmas, as I was told, her arrival at one of our family homes was a flurry of jingling. Her "hired man" would be reining the horse, and the jaunty cutter would have a bright red ribbon flying from the snapper on the whip. Auntie Clara was always dressed a notch fancier than the other women, but she wasn't meaning to be ostentatious about that. She was folksy, and always brought a hamper of small gifts for everybody. After the hired man delivered her, he would jingle home to return for her later.

This went on for a good many years, and there was naturally talk among the women about how Auntie Clara always attended on Christmas but never offered to reciprocate. For the few gewgaws in her hamper, she mulcted a happy holiday and a free feed, and while everybody had entertained Auntie Clara, Auntie Clara never entertained in return. It's possible something of this came to her, some way or other, because there came a year at last when word ran around that everybody in the family would go to Auntie Clara's this year for Christmas.

Which was great, because of all the homes we had, Auntie Clara's was the biggest and the best for a Christmas. It had a fireplace in every room! The kitchen still had the original pioneer fireplace, big enough so a Queen Atlantic cookstove had been set into it, and over the stove the brick oven with its cast-iron door was available and used. The women looked forward to getting the big Christmas dinner in that kitchen, and perhaps brought some goodies not generally included. Auntie Clara, assisted by her "hired woman," had a master big gander ready to roast, and by the time the women unpacked all the baskets, the kitchen table was covered with pies. Some of our very-Low-Churchers were awed to find that Auntie Clara had invited the vicar and his wife, but he was a jolly, bouncy, outgoing sort who soon had everybody at east. So everybody was there and everything seemed to be in good shape when the house caught fire.

Probably the chimney was old enough to have a flaw, and a spark found a way. The wall behind the stove burst out in flame that spread before anybody collected himself. Then the wom

en's outcry brought the men from the parlor, where they had been biding with the children around the tree, and then pails-and pans brought water from the well. There was a busy time, and then suddenly the fire was out. But everything in the kitchen was soaked, as well as sooted, and that table of pies was a sorry mess. Merry Christmas, indeed. . . .

While everybody stood around, mostly in tears, and the vicar was putting his fingers together and saying, "Dear, dear!" Auntie Clara burst out laughing. Not a quiet, ladylike chuckle, but a real riot of hysterics—like a haw-haw-haw. It would certainly be called an unseemly guffaw, on Christmas and at the moment. "Look!" she said, and pushing her wet, smoky hair back from her forehead she splashed across the wet floor and through the debris, towards the range, which was still steaming from the dousing. She reached above the range to open the iron door on the brick oven in the chimney. There, with everybody looking at it, was a crusty beanpot.

So it was. Auntie Clara used her kitchen range for all her cooking except the weekly pot of baked beans. That had to be brought to perfection in the brick oven, where the residual heat persuaded beans in a manner never achieved by any other kind of fire. Everybody knows that, but not everybody has a brick oven. Auntie Clara had started her pot on Christmas eve, intending to let it mull over the holiday, and it would be just right for supper on the 26th, which was a Saturday. And there the beans were, revealed as the only food in the house to survive the blaze.

Auntie Clara found a couple of dry potholders in a drawer, and signaled the vicar to perform. He carried the beanpot from the kitchen towards the parlor, everybody following along behind in the traditional Christmas parade otherwise honoring the bag pudding with its brandy flame and sprig of holly. The regular dishes were now in the kitchen shambles, so the "tea things" were taken down and the beans distributed. That was the Christmas dinner Auntie Clara served to the family that year, and the only Christmas dinner she ever did serve.

My grandfather, who was there, told me it was a truly jolly time. Afterwards, it took several months to clean and restore the kitchen, but that day they just forgot about the mess and enjoyed the tree in the parlor and ate the beans. "Might as well laugh as cry!" Auntie Clara kept saying.

My grandfather said the vicar hesitated when asked to say grace. It was, after all, a *different* situation. But then he recovered, and he held his plate of beans up in front of him, like a sacrificial offering, and he said, "Dear Father—bless these beans; bless them every one!"

37 A Good Night's Sleep

Del Bates, bless him, was the one who got elected to the Maine Legislature from the up-state town of Patten and came down to Augusta with an ingrown disposition about saving money. When he wouldn't go along with "the front office" on a big appropriation, Governor Barrows chided him with, "I'm sure, Mr. Bates, that the good people of Patten had somebody else better than you to send down here to represent them!"

Del said, "They did! They did! But I'm the only one that has a suit of clothes."

Del, too-soon gone and remembered frequently, left me many quotations that are apt off and on, and I love to bounce one of them at my first wife when she tells me about something to do. "Righto!" I say, "I'll take care of that first thing in the morning!" Then I add, "Father." I had to explain this the other day to a friend who heard me add, "Father," and it makes one of the better Del Bates stories.

Del was a life-time clerk for the Great Northern Paper Company, and I first met him decades ago when he was "cock-o'-the-woods" at the Scott Brook camp in the Caucomagomac Lake region. Scott Brook was a big operation and Del was considered the most capable clerk in the company. Of the 150 men in camp, Del was maybe the only one who didn't speak French, almost the only one who spoke English. I was immediately much taken with Del when I saw the Jolly Roger, a white flag with skull and crossbones, flying from his "cockshop" porch. It was an unusual design to find that far in the woods, and it proved Del had whimsy. Over the years Del broke in many a young man as a "pen pusher," or as sometimes designated, a "bean counter." That is, a lumbercamp company clerk—the trade of the legendary Johnny Inkslinger, who was clerk for Paul Bunyan himself. Does anybody recall that Johnny Inkslinger left the crosses off his t's and the dots off his i's and in one winter saved seven barrels of ink? The best Del ever did, he testified, was four barrels. So when Del got an apprentice he would admonish him to keep cool, calm, and collected and never let his work fluster him. Don't get excited! Del said he learned this valuable lesson from his father.

And Del was the living example of the wisdom of this. One hot summer day at Scott Brook Del was sitting in the shade of his camp with his shirt off and a sudden thunder shower dropped a bolt of lightning that struck not ten feet from him. The fuel tanks for the camp's purposes were adjacent, and the one with 2,500 gallons of gasoline was ignited right there, you might say, in Del's lap. The veracity of what happened next is in the excellent history of the Scott Brook operation by R. E. Blodgett, who retired from Great Northern Paper Company employment after a long career in 1989. The book recalls just about everything that happened there in twenty-six years—the longest period of activity of any Maine lumbercamp. Mr. Blodgett says that when the fuel tank began to spout flames from the vent hole on top, Del took immediate notice and clad only in his pants he discreetly withdrew for a distance that was often estimated but never measured. The periphery available for this lucky escape took up twelve townships and parts of seven more. As it turned out, Del's estimate of his necessity was on the high side, because the fire was quickly doused and no damage done. Adelard Gilbert, the *entrepreneur de bois* at Scott Brook, called for a blanket and put it over the vent. The rest of that afternoon and all evening the men discussed the matter, holding themselves lucky, and the next morning Del returned in time for breakfast.

Del's father had been a "walking boss" in the Patten area, where everything in those days centered around lumbering. A walking boss is merely an operations manager who has several camps to look after and walks from one to the other. Except that walking bosses usually had a horse and pung. Del had numberless yarns about his father, and he must have been a remarkable man. He said that his father made no restrictions with his sons about Saturday night pleasuring, but he made a rule that the last boy in bed Saturday night had to milk the cows Sunday morning. Del told me, "We boys never knew how Father knew, but he always did." In time Del's brothers found work, but his father felt Del had the makings of a good camp clerk and steered him accordingly. Later, Del studied accounting at Bentley in Boston, but as a mere lad he accompanied his father from camp to camp and absorbed experience. One of Northern's managers told me once, "If I have to set up a camp from scratch and can have my pick of company clerks—he'd be Del Bates."

So in his early days of becoming a bean counter—the camp clerk keeps track of commissary inventory and knows if cook has enough dry beans—Del arrived at a remote camp with his father. His father was explaining this and that, and Del was doing his very best to learn his lessons. He was eager to please his father and show how smart he was. It happened that this camp had but one vacant bunk, so Del and his father would have to share it. This camp was at Six-Mile in Masardis Surplus, at the head of the Masardis loghaul, and if you look at the map you'll see that alternate accommodations were at a distance. Del turned in, and after discussing matters with the camp foreman, his father joined him. Del was still in high school, and not quite a big boy yet, but things were tight. The bunkhouse quieted down, and the snoring began. I can hear Del now:

"Father went right to sleep, and after a time I did, too. But boy-fashion I was wanting to please the old man, so in my sleep I suppose I got to pondering on things he set me to do, and I came up fitful and restless. I must have churned a good deal, because two-three times he'd poke me and say, 'Stiddy! Stiddy!' But I kept on squirming, and finally in my dreams I must have got things squared away, because all at once I sat up in the bunk, still sound asleep, and I calls out, 'Yes, father! I'll take care of that first thing in the morning!'

"But my father had had enough by then and he had a different idea. 'Nothin' doing!' he yells back at me so that he woke up every man in camp. 'You go take care of it right now!'

"And he kicked me out of bed. I sat up in a chair until daybreak, the longest night of my life. And my father never said one word afterwards about kicking me out of bed. But the next morning, after we'd had breakfast and were in the pung going to the next camp, he said, 'Son, never take your work to bed with you. Leave it on your desk. It'll be there next day. Most important thing of all is a good night's sleep.' "

38 Consider Fidelia—No AARP, She!

There's no better way to show what's happened to us than to tell about Grammie Curtis. I reflect on her every time I hear the words "charity" and "welfare" and "underprivileged" and even "destitute" and "needy." Grammie Curtis was attached to our family back in the 1920s in a manner the unfolding century removed from our uses—I guess society has no place for a Grammie Curtis today. She was never a grandmother to us, but she could have been no closer as a blood relative. She was a grandmother to some youngsters out of state, but in Grammie Curtis's time of need her own folks were distant both in miles and interest. So she came to live with us.

It was her right name—Fidelia. She had been a Ward from Wardtown, which was a prestigious section of our town given over, mostly, to Wards. Fidelia had married Orrin Curtis while she was still in her teens, and it had been a fine marriage. She was devoted to taking care of Orrin, and he was devoted to letting her. Today the Feminists deplore that kind of slavish downgrading in wedlock, but Grammie Curtis knew no different and stayed happy. So did Orrin.

I think we never knew what Orrin's lifework had been, but he had retired from it and did little more than attend a small garden, which he kept orderly and very productive. Our town was loaded with retired sea captains, and I think we may have surmised that Orrin had made some money in that bygone profession. Most of our retired sea captains had made their piles before they were twenty-five and thirty, and Orrin could have done that, too. Maybe he had some bonds in a western railroad. The thing that should have told us otherwise was the house— Orrin's wasn't one of the four-square shipyard homes of the retired master mariners. His sat amongst such, but it was late Victorian and didn't match. Anyway, when Orrin came to the end of his book he didn't have much of anything, and Fidelia got that house and that was it. She sold it, but then had no place to live. It was never in her mind to "call on," either to her distant kin or to the town, so she moved in with us, next door, and stayed for many years.

We did have a big house, built by the shipwrights for a sea captain, but we'd bought it—it wasn't inherited. A big house requires care. So our mother, who never really, in so many words, invited Grammie Curtis, was glad for help with the housework and family, and Grammie Curtis took over. She was first up in the morning, starting breakfast to get us children off to school, and then she did her daily chores with laundry and cleaning, darning and dressmaking, whatever. She carried table scraps to the hens and picked up the eggs. She set the milk and churned, and before long she was reminding me to put on a clean shirt.

Grammie Curtis had not been favored with beauty, and had no more feminine charm than a stepladder. Her feet were at least size 14 (men's) and she wore lumberman's felt larrigans while doing housework. Her toes turned out plentifully, so she walked like a side-wheeler steamboat—with determined stride. She had side-wheeled our sleeping cat in passing so poor Paragot was punch-drunk and no longer spry enough to get out of her way. But Grammie Curtis had a heart the size of a bushel basket and her love ran over. She was all but humorless, and while our family was well given to merry quips, badinage, pleasantries, and witticisms we never made jokes with or about Grammie Curtis. She may have smiled, but I never knew her to laugh.

In her years at our house she was ever faithful to her duties, and her duties were simply to work her keep and not be a burden. And these duties she established herself, because they were never set down by my mother. The ancient adage runs that no home can have two mistresses, and it was amazing that Grammie Curtis could assume so much authority and never disturb the harmony. My mother, of course, played her part in that harmony. Even in those days when neighborly kindness was fairly common, we ran into people now and then who didn't understand about Grammie Curtis. One Sunday we had callers who stayed for supper, and from the way Grammie Curtis operated the stove, arranged the table, and brought on the food the visitors assumed she was domestic help. I guess in those days we wouldn't have called anybody domestic help—maybe "hired woman" is better.

But when Grammie Curtis took her place at table and began serving the chicken, doubts arose. And when she tinkled on the water glass with her spoon and said grace, there was indeed wonder. Who was she? And when Grammie Curtis told my mother to be careful and not spill any cranberry sauce on the clean tablecloth, confusion set in for real. After the meal, and before leaving, the visitors tactfully asked Mother to explain, which she did by saying, "Oh, she's Grammie Curtis."

After a time some relative of Grammie Curtis, down in New Jersey, made it known that she had a place there if she wanted to come, and our house was torn for weeks as the options were debated and Grammie Curtis made her decision. She elected to go to New Jersey, her main reason being that we children were grown and Mother didn't need so much help around the house and "an extra mouth to feed." We never saw her again, and since she didn't live long we always supposed she was unhappy at the change. Never once, in all the years Grammie Curtis lived with us and took care of us did it enter our heads that she came to us poor and in need; that she was a welfare case; and that we were giving of our substance.

39 A Better Race—and Fun!

U sing approved methods, I polled my ten close friends at random, and they all agreed that the big yacht races for the America's Cup are just as much fun as a good toothache. They all, like me, wonder why the newspapers and magazines go gaga over the foolishness and shove detailed analyses down the readers' throats when everybody would much prefer a friendly dog fight. The people who build the boats and race them seem always to be well-heeled bastards who don't know what else to do with their money, and they are always mad about something and finding fault, and no matter how smart they are nobody can get along with them. Although three of my ten friends disagreed about their being bastards—they think they're sons-of-bitches.

Yet every time an America's Cup contest comes up, every reporter in the business begins talking about sheer and yawing and luffing and starboard tacks, and seems to think anybody who has fifty cents to spend for something to read believes in yachting as two notches above religion, home, mother, school teachers, the Republican Party, and God, in that order. I, personally and without prompting, can remember when Sir Thomas Lipton was about to race one of his *Shamrocks* against either the

Resolute or the *Vanitie*, whichever came first, and in all those years I never knew of a respectable citizen who gave a hoot one way or the other.

The finest development of the sailing vessel came in the late 1800s when Maine shipwrights in Maine shipyards built the downeaster, a vessel that sailed from Maine with a Maine crew and usually a Maine master, and improving on the clipper extended the age of sail into the age of steam for another three decades. If the toy boats used in the America's Cup nonsense had any true connection with seafaring, however remote, Maine coastal people would like to know what it is. And if any newspaper and periodical (the *New Yorker*, even, has profound articles on the Cup exercises) cares enough to do the very best, I suggest a short item about our annual chowder race in Friendship hah-b'h.

A hundred years ago lobstering, seining, and even setting trawls, was done out of Friendship Harbor by sail. There developed in Muscongus Bay several variations of the sloop that were designed on purpose for fishing. The first requirement was that they could be sailed by one man, two at the most. Then they had to handle well—a man hauling lobster traps should be able to leave the tiller while he 'tended gear, and the sloop should behave herself. She should "jog" well and come about neatly. She should have cargo space for bringing home the catch, and if she had a "well" she shouldn't be sluggish with it. A well was a built-in tank of sea water to keep lobsters fresh. And after all the duty features, Maine preference insisted that she look good. The Friendship Sloop almost sailed herself, served every need, and she was pretty as a pail of new milk when she rounded Franklin Island and headed home. A few photographs can be found which show Friendship Harbor in those days, a hair-brush of sloop masts, gaff rigged and sturdy for sea work, trim vessels waiting on the morrow's tide and a breeze. Once a year, at Labor Day time, the fishermen of Friendship turned from their labors at sea and had a day of "pleasurin'." That's the word—the lobsterman, today, who puts in his week hauling his traps and gives

Sunday over to taking his family down to Otter Island for a picnic will tell you he's pleasurin'. The pleasuring of the Friendshippers, who had the town to themselves in those days before summer-complaints, included a race that seems to have turned out every boat in the harbor that had a rag to hoist. Pity the motion picture and the TV were so long a-coming. We have no visual records of those encounters. Conceding that the men at the tillers were the world's masters of the sailing art, and that their boats were designed by local craftsmen for perfection in home waters, those races were certainly something to confound the rich bastards of the yacht clubs. What would a reporter on the New York *Times* know about a boat, anyway?

When motors were perfected, a good many of those sloops got one shoved inboard, and under power continued to fish until they fell apart. Others were beached out to suffer and die, and there developed new styles of lobster boats even to the glass hulls that need only to be "finished off," which Friendship craftsmen will do. That is, Friendship fishing no longer depended on sail, and except for an occasional after sailcloth at the stern-sheets to "stiddy," no Friendship workboat will show you a sail. The annual fisherman's race became historical, and waited a few years for a new generation to revive it.

Each year, on the Labor Day weekend, Friendship Harbor stages the annual "Chowder Race," and there is no record whatever that anybody ever found fault, criticized, belittled, argued, took offense, or put on a big show of American's Cup hatred for humanity. Nobody even has to belong to a yacht club. As for me, myself, I became involved by the happenstance of possession. Understand, I am not a boater, and my flotation experience has been in a canoe on the Allagash River and a number of assorted fresh-water ponds. I didn't know until just lately what a Friendship Sloop was; truth is, I didn't know what a sloop was. As a guest, unlicensed to touch anything on board, I had gone "down below" a few times with Cappy on his *Blossom*, lobs'trin', but Cappy wouldn't know a jib from an outside reach, as no more would I. I expect Cappy didn't have enough cloth aboard *Blossom* to wave if he needed help. So I was a most unlikely candidate for involvement in the annual Friendship Harbor Chowder Race, and was astonished when I was asked to be a member of the race committee. This is not an unimportant position, and it is a high honor. It amounts to being regent of the New York Yacht Society, or First Lord of the Admiralty. And it turned out it was not an invitation extended because everybody else had already declined. They really needed me. Very much. I was the only person anybody knew about that owns a saluting cannon.

Mine was made by Winchester in the 1800s, and has reposed unused as an antique except that every fourth of July I gave a bang with it when we raise Old Glory. It has been difficult to get ten-gauge shells for it, because as saluting guns declined the need for ammunition kept pace. I've heard that the demand for saluting cannon, lulled for many years, has lately increased with new interest in yacht races and Winchester is again making them. Meantime, the Friendship Chowder Race had a vacancy, and I had a cannon. It is a dandy little banger, a miniature of a Battle of Gettysburg original, and I wouldn't take money for it. As things go now, the annual Chowder Race is the last hooraw of the summer for all those good Friendshippers who pack up and go home on Labor Day. While the descendants of true Friendship fishermen pay no heed, everybody else turns out and races in keen intensity for the only trophy—no big and prestigious "mug," this, but a can of Snow's clam chowder.

I found the race committee is well provided for. A considerable stinkpot named *Maude* is more than adequate, with head and galley and such, and comfortable deck furniture. Maude, herself, is a local artist in oils and water colors and teaches at the Farnsworth—comparable to the Louvre and the Tate—and she presides at race committee meetings in an affable manner and with malice towards none. Her husband, except when preparing refreshments, runs the boat, in that order. Several members are designated as spotters, and have binoculars, clip-boards, and fourteen-ounce tumblers. There is one member who keeps run

ning signal flags up and down, and another who is the timer. Then there are several other people. We assemble well in advance of the starting time, which is noon, and after everybody is served the boat is moved off to its mooring, which becomes one end of the starting line. I arrange my cannon, making sure it is tied so I won't lose it overboard, and adjust my lunch. They couldn't hold the race without me, but the timer tells me when to shoot. The first gun is at 11:50 A.M., EDST, and the timer informs me thus: "Ready—five, four, three, two, one—PULL!" We give another blast at 11:55, and then comes the starting gun at high twelve. Then the boats go down the harbor and we all eat lunch.

You can see this is all very different from the big race for the America's Cup. Nobody has found fault, and no papers have been served in a big international lawsuit. Nothing untoward has diminished the serenity except that when the warning gun went off Maude spilled her sauce, a mishap of only momentary importance. When the starting gun goes off, everything in Muscongus Bay that can put up some cloth is just about three feet (half a fathom) from the starting line and you can just betcha it's a far more stirring sight than to see a couple of jiggy rigs and nothing else to look at. We always have a couple of schooners, and then a bunch of sloops, but the race is open to anything, and in and out will be a dozen or so sailfish—a sailfish is an ironing board with a tablecloth. Beautiful competitors are the

Friendship Cats—a distinctive local catboat lately revived by Doug Lash and one of his brothers, but Doug isn't sure which brother. You can get one for right around $5,000, which is a good deal cheaper than a lot of other things. They sail like a dream, and none has ever capsized in a Chowder Race the way the sailfishes do. When we have a good breeze the Chowder Race doesn't last long, but with a slack wind the committee likes to cruise down along the islands and linger over lunch. But we have to be back on mooring, because the starting line is also the finish line, and I have to blow a blast when the winner passes the mark. Handicaps? No.

The Friendship Chowder Race has no grievance committee. If you get mad about something, keep it to yourself. Nobody's interested. True, with schooners and sloops and sailfishes and catboats and knockabouts and sailing dories and cutters and sometimes the Viking vessel from Outward Bound (and the Coast Guard dope control) all scrambling for position, a grievance is by no means difficult to imagine. The philosophy is that the Friendship Chowder Race is meant to be a good time, and how could you have a good time with everybody finding fault?

The Chowder Race "rain date" is next year.

40 Expressing Thanksgiving Joy

The railroads went sour here in Maine some years back, and we have a persistent claque of choo-choo buffs who clamor for the state to resume service on certain defunct tracks that serve no purpose now except to show where the lines were. People who really liked trains, and I did, will shrug that off, and while I can't tell you all the reasons for choo-choo failures, I know one of them was the Freeport Poultry Show. Let me shed light on the unhappiness:

Poultry was a Maine specialty, and for an excellent good reason. In the days of sail, food for a passage was always the first consideration. But when the eager Maine sea captains began taking their families on voyages, an extra dimension was added and there came about certain refinements. For one thing—fresh eggs. The answer was a chicken coop by the taffrail, and Mrs. Captain would step out each morning to fetch in the eggs so the seagoing children might have their decent breakfasts. When a hen laid down, so to speak, on her responsibilities and passed the day in reluctant production, she'd go into the stewpot. Such a hen had to be replaced, and in the next port of call the mate would be instructed to find a few replacement hens, who would lay eggs all the way home. In no time at all, every barnyard in Maine had hens from all over the world, and Mainers became the foremost authorities on poultry. There is on record the matter of a black Minorca rooster for the Widow Proctor of Pennellville, whose flock of fine hens was widowed by a fox that came in the night and murdered their husband. A rooster is not necessary when it comes to laying eggs, but unfertilized eggs never hatch, and the Widow Proctor put a notice in the post office to the effect that she needed a Black Minorca rooster, and she would be grateful if somebody going to the Mediterranean would be kind enough to fetch one home. The Minorca is not too big a bird, as hens go, and they lay eggs like the dickens. So within six months the Widow Proctor got sixty-seven roosters. That's the way things were.

It was the same with cats. Any time a Maine sea captain saw a cat in a far place that he thought his wife might like to have, he'd bring it home. You name any kind of a cat, and you'll find one of them somewhere in Maine today.

Freeport was a seafaring town. Rufus Cushing built over a hundred deep-water craft in his time, and launched his 67th on his 67th birthday. The day came when you could call almost any elderly man in Freeport "Cap'n," and he'd earned it. So Freeport came to have all the classical poultry from all over the world, and the Freeport Poultry Show was as good as any anywhere. Fact is, a Freeporter once shipped a rooster all the way to Melbourne, Australia, to an International Poultry Congress, and the rooster won "best in show." The man used to tell how he offered the rooster at sale for fifty dollars, but he didn't sell, so the family ate him. A fifty-dollar Sunday dinner in those days was high living.

The annual exhibition of the Freeport Poultry Association came between Thanksgiving and Christmas, and the town hall was full of wire cages in which you could find, somewhere, every kind of barnyard fowl known. There were other poultry shows elsewhere, and all the county fairs used to stage them, but the Freeport show had the prestige, and anybody at a distance who was trying to build up a name for his breeding stock would go after a prize at Freeport. So each year a lot of birds came by railway express to the Freeport hen show, adding to the home-town birds exhibited by Freeporters from their old sea-captain beginnings.

Now you have the background. The Freeport Poultry Show ceased around 1927, when the beautiful old breeds gave over to the new hydrids bred for the new era. Feathers lost their beauty in the utilitarian desire for heft and easy-clean plucking in the mechanized abattoirs. And along about 1940, or so, my wife and I were riding around on the back roads of Vermont, and we came upon a turkey farm. Here was an entire hillside given over to thousands of turkeys. They would soon be marched away to be made ready for Thanksgiving dinners. "Let's buy one for Dad!" said my companion, who was also my wife, and it seemed like a fine idea. The family gathered in those days with Father and Mother to turkey together, and here was a chance to provide the chief ingredient. We drove up the driveway to the house, and found a pleasant woman who said yes, that she'd sell a bird.

As for my father, a live turkey-tom would be no problem. Dad grew up on a farm, and very early he taught me to pluck and draw a hen, showing me first how to tell if she were laying. No sense in cutting down a layer. The tom we bought from the Vermont woman stood thirty-two inches tall and was in proportion throughout. This was important, because live creatures offered to the railroads for shipment had to have cages in which they could stand. Cruelty to dumb animals. So we paid for our tom and told the woman we'd be back, and we drove into Montpelier to find a lumberyard. Having a crate big enough, we now put Tom in it and conducted him to the Plainfield station of the Montpelier & Wells River Railroad, where Wesley Willard was the resident agent and put in his time between two trains a day. They were the same train—eastbound and westbound. We told Wesley we would like to prepay our turkey to Freeport, Maine.

Wesley relieved himself of a few Calvin Coolidge remarks, asking what these foolish tourists would think up next, and so on, and he said, "Make him stand up!"

"He can stand up," I said. "I measured him."

Tom was, of course, one of the whimsys where price doesn't matter. Cost what it might, we wanted to surprise Dad with a twenty-seven-pound Vermont turkey all a-gobble, and we let Wes run his course with sarcasm and terse Vermont humor. Wes went behind his wicket and sat at his desk and began to thumb through a tariff book. He found a reference, and he reached down another book. He got down a third, and then went back to the first. Tom, all wrought up over the joy of moving to Maine, gobbled in his cage on the platform wagon and made a touse that resounded up and down the Winooski River Valley amazingly. Wes scribbled on a sheet of paper. At last he closed the books, stood up, and said, "It comes to forty-eight cents."

Then he said, "Dammit—that *can't* be right!"

"Does seem a little on the light side," I said.

Wes went out and looked at Tom in his cage, hefted one side of the crate, and then put the crate on the scales again. "Let me try that again," he said.

Back to the tariff schedules, and again, "Forty-eight it is," he said. Then he said, "That's just plain stupid, and it can't be right. Just under a hundred pounds, crate and all, and five different railroads, and every man that handles the thing has to check the food and water. Forty-eight cents?"

Wesley went over the tariffs again. I surmised an answer, but I didn't offer to enlighten Wes. It cost forty-eight cents to ship the biggest tom turkey in the world from Plainfield, Vermont, to Freeport, Maine. Wes made out the waybill, waggling his head and saying, "Forty-eight cents!"

Well, it was our old Freeport Poultry Show. In the wonderful days that were, when the railroads had no problems and even the conductors smiled, long before the Maine Truck Owners' Association and Henry Ford, and before the Good Roads Advocates, the railroads had established a special tariff on live poultry to and from Freeport—and extra special for return handling. Once a year a couple of carloads of show-birds would take advantage of this, and the rest of the year nobody sent barnyard fowl to Freeport. A generation had passed, the Freeport Poultry Show was musty and forgotten in the archives of the Freeport Historical Society, and Wes Willard hadn't been informed of any changes.

So in a way the railroads contributed to their own early demise by not paying attention. If I had sent Old Tom Thanksgiving to Yarmouth or Brunswick—two towns adjacent to Freeport—his passage would have cost $13.80. So what about these buffs who think a railroad will pay if they revive it?

41 A Pinch for Bucky

Who's buried in Grant's tomb? All right, now tell us who is buried in the Taj Mahal. No help from the audience, please! Have I made my point? The Shah Jahan, back in the 17th century, had the beautiful mausoleum at Agra, India, built as a tomb and memorial for his favorite wife—Mumtaz Mahall. She and the Shah share the shack in a vault under the high dome, and all I'm trying to say is that everybody knows about the Taj Mahal and nobody can tell you the wife's name. That, as Humpty Dumpty probably said, is glory for you! What's the point of having the most beautiful memorial in the world if nobody remembers you? On the other hand, I don't even know where Bucky is buried, and I can tell you his name and I think of him every week, and while he's long gone from this brief world of ours, he'll never be forgotten. That, too, is glory for you.

Lester Buck was a registered Maine guide at Kennebago Lake for years, and had a string of loyal "sports" who came every summer and were considered "stiddy" customers. Bucky guided only for fishing on Kennebago Lake, and never guided for deer hunting and he wouldn't walk a trail. Not everybody knew this, whereby hangs a parable which I'll get to, but Bucky had but one leg. I know which leg he'd lost, but I'm not going to tell you. It was back in his youth when he worked in the carbarn at Litchfield for the cross-country electric trolley line known as the Androscoggin & Kennebec. Bucky himself never knew how the mishap came about, but he lost a leg under a car wheel. With a wooden leg he managed, and he was able to guide from the seat of a Rangeley boat. He walked well enough so his slight limp didn't betray his lack, but he kept out of the woods. Being guided by Bucky was to be honored. The day's routine for one of his sports was to have a good breakfast with Bucky up at the guides' camp, bacon and eggs and toast and camp coffee, and then go down the lake for the morning fishing. At noon, Bucky would put in at one of the lunchgrounds and, using trout from the morning catch, perfect a magnificent trout chowder which took more than a little time. A trout chowder should simmer into its maximum. One of Bucky's gambits to amuse his sports was to go down to these lunchgrounds early in the spring and tame some deer. Bucky "had a way" with animals, and this didn't take long. He'd put a few crumbled saltine crackers on a stump, and come back the next day to leave a few more. The deer, usually does about to lamb, would find the crackers. The rest was easy; Bucky would get them to come at his call, and along in June there would be fawns to come out with them. "Funny we ain't seen no deer," Bucky would say to his sport at lunchtime, "maybe I better call some." So he'd husky-like in his throat, the way a mama-deer talks to the fawn, and out from the pucker-brush would burst Bucky's tame deer. Nobody can compute the amount of money Eastman Kodak made selling film to snap-shoot Bucky's deer.

The parable of his wooden leg depended on his guiding somebody who didn't know he had one. When the trout weren't coming for his sport, Bucky would begin his monolog about the efficacy of the silver doctor as against the grey ghost, and why a nymph goes good inshore but won't raise a thing ten feet farther out, and the sport would listen as the pupils listened to Aristotle. Bucky would at last get to the question, "What do you have on?"

That is, what is the name of the fly on your leader? Sometimes the sport would know one fly from another, but Bucky would say, "Lemme look at it!"

"No wonder," he'd say, "no intelligent fish would touch that. Here, let me tie on something else."

Then would follow an idle moment. The sport would slacken his line so Bucky could reach the leader, and would sit on the thwart watching as Bucky changed the fly—his rod across his knees. Bucky would get his great hunting knife from the sheath on his belt, cut the fly off the leader, thread the new fly, tie off the new end of the leader, and then trim the excess with his knife. He'd have the knife in one hand, using the other to inspect the new fly. Then he'd toss the new fly overboard, ram the end of his hunting knife through his pants into his wooden leg, reach for the oars, and say, "There, try that."

The knife would stick there, vibrating, as Bucky began to row again, and the sport would never know if he should throw up or jump overboard. He would be brought out of his trance by Bucky's, "Well, go ahead and fish—no point to my rowing if you don't fish."

When Kennebago had frost around the edges and the fishing season was over, Bucky would come down from Kennebago and take a room in Lewiston for the winter. He had no family that anybody knew about, and we suspected his was a lonely winter. So I'd drive up now and then and bring Bucky down to our place for Saturday night supper, and a few games of cribbage. Bucky liked his baked beans, and he was hard to beat at cribbage. I'd drive him back after the evening, and he was grateful. The first Saturday night that we entertained Bucky, he came to the table and in turn helped himself to a plate of beans. There was a platter of buttermilk biscuits, a cabbage salad, and the usual with-its of the Saturday night feast. Bucky lifted the first forkful of beans to his lips, chewed and swallowed, and he looked at my wife. She, like all cooks, cherishes a compliment, and because she does bake a good bean she expected one. Bucky said, "Dorothy—you didn't put in no ginger!"

"I never put ginger in my beans."

"You should always put ginger in your beans. It's uncivilized to leave out the ginger. But not too much!" Bucky added. "Just a pinch. These would be extra fine beans if they just had a pinch of ginger."

Since that evening, our family beans have always had that pinch of ginger, and they have always been extra fine beans. The next time Bucky came for Saturday night supper and cribbage, he spoke highly of the beans, and he never again had cause to complain. Every Saturday morning, at our house, the beanpot is made ready for the oven, and just before the cover is set in place my wife says, like one reciting a ritual, ". . . and a pinch of ginger for Bucky."

Bucky is long gone, and I have no idea where he's buried. But he's remembered, and now—once again—who is it that's memorialized by the Taj Mahal?

42 College by the Back Hall

Grandson William decided to do his college down in Rebel country, and I got a letter from him that said he was having trouble finding some work for the summer, and was obliged to take a part-time job that paid only $175 a week. I set out to, and then decided not to tell him how I had a high-school summer job that paid me $3 a day for shoveling gravel from seven to five into the tipcarts of the town highway crew. That figured to $18 a week, except that I didn't get paid on rainy days. Then, too, along in August the appropriation ran out and because I was temporary help I got "laid off." Between that and school I filled in as a haymaker for George Bartoll at $1 a day, but George did give me my dinner. I didn't tell William, either, that in my time college tuition was $200 a year. And I didn't tell him any "back hall" stories, either.

The back halls of innumerable Maine vacation resorts helped thousands of boys and girls to afford college right up to the time Uncle Sam's accursed thirst for gold slid such resorts into limbo. Meantime, of course, Uncle Sam was giving loud lip service to education. That's true. There were other reasons for the decline of the Maine vacation resort, but the *coup de grâce* was the IRS decision to collect a withholding tax on tips. Those old "camps" were a thing unto themselves and there was no possible way to squeeze them into the averages of government forms. They didn't compute, you might say. On top of wages and hours regulations that couldn't in any way be adjusted to comply with wilderness customs, the withholding tax on tips made just too much book-keeping that couldn't be done anyway. One by one, and just about unanimously, the owners and operators of Maine's wood-land resort camps decided to do away with dining halls, and waitresses, and without a dining hall there could be no camp.

The wages paid for "seasonal help" at those resort camps weren't much. The guides and cooks and most adults did all right, but the youngsters who came to do much of the work depended on tips. Guests, most of whom were well-to-do from "the city," understood that, and acted accordingly. The girls who waited on table got their uniforms and a pittance, but the "guests" were generous when it came time to depart. Same with the choreboy. It was scandalous the way camp owners found boys to work fourteen hours a day, or more, right through the sum-mer at maybe ten dollars a week. But the choreboy had to come in every morning and light a fire in the guest's Franklin fire-place, and he had to feed the dog and get a newspaper and keep the woodbox full and see that the automobile was stabled, and put up the net on the tennis court, and by the time gratified guests had fulfilled their days they were glad to make him pros-perous, and if you get tips enough you can afford to work for nothing.

In the heyday of choreboy prosperity, Maine was dry. The

Neal Dow influence lingered, and it was a sad surprise to many a guest to arrive with a heavy thirst and be told that Maine enjoyed prohibition. Such guests, in a whisper, were told to consult the choreboy. When Maine was indeed lawfully parched, the proximity of Quebec Province was a boon. Any choreboy could walk fourteen miles, and the customary cache was the icehouse. Somewhere in the sawdust that kept the pond ice from thawing, the choreboy had his secret place with a supply of about anything you might require. His prices were the same as he paid in Quebec, with a reasonable mark-up to cover wear and tear on his boots, and the tip was at the guest's discretion. Being a choreboy at a respectable Maine vacation lodge was as good as a license to steal. And waitresses were in that same bracket.

Uncle Sam didn't know anything about running a summer camp. Vacations don't keep industrial hours. The camp owners rightly allowed that the guest–waitress relationship was none of their business, and they wisely decided the waitresses weren't about to divulge how they were tipped, anyway. If Louise didn't level with the IRS, go after Louise—but the IRS said Oh-No, you make Louise tell you, and you collect it, and you pay us. Thus the IRS put the Maine summer camp out of business, and made it that much more difficult for an energetic Maine boy or girl to get an education.

The big thing about working in a Maine vacation camp for your "found" and tips was the good fun it was. People were coming from far places to pay hefty money for fresh air and fine food and scenery and here you were getting all that for nothing and making money on the side. The "back hall," where the help ate and had their privacy away from the guests, was a place no guests, however well heeled, could rightly invade, and the guests never knew about that side of their vacations. Although one camp owner told me one time about a Mr. Adams, also from Philadelphia, who found out about the back hall and yearned. It came about by mistake. Mr. Adams always came for opening day and enjoyed a week's fishing right after ice-out, and then he would come again in August with his family for three weeks.

In some places an "opening note" may be the first music at a concert, or maybe the first warble of a spring hermit thrush, but in Maine summer vacation lingo it is the ninety-day money advanced by a bank so the owner can open for the season and pay his bills until the guests begin paying him. All the buildings have to be cleaned after the winter, the bedding brought out and aired, the beds made, towels put in the racks, the water turned on, and all the woodboxes filled. The kitchen crew will stack supplies on the shelves, check everything from pepper to pickles, and the waitresses are all on hand to help. The dockboy gets the boats ready, tests the struggle-strings on all the outboards, and distributes the oars and paddles. And so on. All is bustle and confusion, pretty much, and everything flows to the day, coming up, when the first guests will arrive and the season is on. The "opening note" will be paid off, with interest, before Labor Day.

So this Mr. Adams made a mistake, and in he comes all heifered up over his first trout, and he's three days early. Mr. Adams is too good a guest to abuse, so everybody makes shift, and here is Mr. Adams under foot and everybody trying to get ready for opening without offending him. Mr. Adams, when told he was welcome if he'd do for himself and eat in the back hall, seemed dubious about that, as if he felt it demeaning. A guest of his repute and means, let's say, shouldn't be asked to dine with the help. But Mr. Adams recognized that he had no choice, and he accepted his lot. He then went down the lake, to whip the waters.

Come suppertime, the famished Mr. Adams stepped into the back hall by the back door, entering a domain he knew nothing whatever about, and he was greeted in almost a rowdy manner by Myrtle Sheidow, who was the back hall boss and in charge of opening-day affairs. "Bigod, Mr. Adams," said Myrtle, "we begun to think you warn't coming! Get your trout? How many hamburg patties can you down? Would you like the fried eggs?" She pointed around at the "help," one by one, and Mr. Adams was introduced. "Sit over here by me," said Myrtle, "and see you behave yourself!"

Mr. Adams thus became one of the few summer camp guests who ever saw, and enjoyed, a Maine back hall in action. He was taught to play cribbage. After supper the squeezebox and the fiddle and the mouth organ were brought out, and Pete Nadeau taught Mr. Adams the old Quebec sugar-house dance where a man jumps back and forth over a broomstick.

The upshot was that when camp was opened, and Mr. Adams could begin eating in the dining room, he said if nobody minded he'd like to keep on with the back hall. Myrtle tactfully explained to him that except as a makeshift this couldn't be done—that in this world some things just aren't right and that in a camp a guest has to keep his place. Sorry. Mr. Adams said he understood. He was always generous with tips—putting many a Maine young lady through college until Uncle Sam butted in and made it illegal.

43 They're Good for You!

A friend who will probably cross me off her list recently wrote inquiring if we folks in Maine salute the glad springtime with a feed of dandelion greens, as they do along the Main Line. She says dandelion greens are delicious, but instead of brutally boiling the things as we do in our northern iggerance, they eat them raw with a relish of hot sauce. This is a good thing to know, and it made me think of our daughter Kathryn when she was a tyke and spurned the lobster at the Poland Spring

Hotel. The big Poland Spring House burned flat in 1975, so we are concerned with a spurn of some time ago. The place wasn't far from our home, so we would go there to dine now and then, and it was a great place to inculcate the amenities into the habits of the children. Poland Spring catered to wealthy guests who came to rejuvenate their frayed edges and go home ready to face another year with the facts of quiet desperation. Nobody came into the dining room in sneakers and T-shirt. With the pure water from Poland Spring ever present, the resort put together a vacation package never exceeded at other spas and resorts, and the huge dining room spared nothing in the way of cates and dainties for the well-heeled and fastidious. The kitchens never did anything wrong. We knew the head waiter and he usually beckoned his own wife to serve our table. We also knew Charlie Conners, who managed the resort in its last days of opulent grandeur, and while we were eating Charlie would always come to our table for a visit, and to pat the children on their heads. The children always responded to the elegance of the place, and minded their manners. Nothing untoward ever disturbed the serenity of our dining out thus until the evening Kathryn decided to have the lobster.

She was just school age, pigtailed and perky, but at table at Poland Spring she kept the aplomb of the Queen's Housekeeper, and she enunciated her desires in turn and returned the seven-page menu to the waitress with dignified charm and a gracious smile. The waitress returned to the kitchens. Charm and dignity—pity such attributes are long lost and bygone—much of them died with the dining room at Poland Spring. The waitress never (never) brought in the food. It came on a silver tray the size of Galahad's shield, high on the hand of a liveried busboy who marched with the stately tread of a Roman century exercising in Gaul. Behind the boy came the waitress, keeping step and radiant as a queen about to be crowned. They were met at the table by the head waiter, who superintended the lowering of the tray, making sure every amenity was impeccably correct, and efficiently approving everything. The arrival of food at a Poland Spring table was something to see, like a sunset over Lake Louise, and everybody in the dining room would watch, politely restraining an urge to applaud. So the lobster, that evening, was placed before Kathryn just as nectar and ambrosia would be placed before Juno high on sacred Olympus and there was heard immediately throughout the dining room our daughter's clear, piping statement of fact, "That's not the way my mother cooks it!"

The pouring of a hot sauce over raw dandelion greens is a splendid idea, entirely compatible with the dominant Maine opinion that dandelion greens need all the help they can get. Being better supplied than Philadelphia with native goodies and an understanding of what to do with them, we hold back considerably in making dandelion greens a vernal delight. We have fiddleheads, and shore goosers, winter-cured parsnips, and even rhubarb, and we are not obliged to use dandelion greens. We even have people who come right out and say dandelion greens aren't fit to eat. But if one must eat the things, a hot sauce on the raw foliage is certainly better than the two-hour boil that makes the kitchen smell like washday—the aroma of who threw the overalls in Mrs. Murphy's chowder? After the two-hour boil, our recipe runs, the dandelion greens can be hove to the hens and the Maine family will rejoice to greet the springtime with some red flannel hash and a dropped egg. Otherwise, if one desires to mortify the flesh, the dandelion greens that have been boiled for two hours with a chunk of salt pork may be annointed well with ninety-score butter and a healthy splash of undiluted cider vinegar. This keeps the dandelion greens from tasting too much like dandelion greens and is a good thing. Fast food from McChicky and a couple of garlic submarines also helps the sun cross the line.

We had a maternal uncle who was accounted peculiar in a number of ways, and it was his whim to perpetuate certain traditions, one of them the annual springtime feed of dandelion greens. He'd dig the things and clean them and wash them again, and pick them over, and then he'd boil them for two hours with a piece of salt pork. He also liked sugar pies and tomato mincemeat and vinegar pies and dried apples, and things like that which used to be important in his boyhood. Crazy as a coot. Uncle Lem would eat about anything. When he'd sit down to celebrate the coming of spring with a big soup plate of boiled dandelion greens, he always plastered them with hot mustard, molasses, and mint jelly. He said that helped.

44 A Good Looking Chick

Over the years I have found the ladies congenial and I've loved 'em, and none has ever considered me a mortal enemy. Thus new-day Women's Lib doesn't cause me any undue alarm, and if that's what the dear things want, so be it! I do wish, just as reciprocal common courtesy, somebody would tell me how to pronounce "Ms." There's no such word, and I've never heard anybody say it, and when I ask some feminist about that they give me that male chauvinist look which skewers me against the wall and leaves me unworthy of further notice. By the way, why doesn't some nasty man write a letter to the editors about *male* chauvinism? What gives the ladies this privilege? Any chauvinist is a man. Got to be. The feminine would be chauviniste. Look it up. Gracious! Well, all that aside, I got a letter from a gracious lady not long ago, and she upbraids me in the finest Women's Lib fashion because I called Cynthia a chick. Cynthia works in the bank and she has my interest at heart. I like Cynthia. The last thing I would do is cause Cynthia any woe. So I was agog with remorse at the imputation, and I looked back in the book and sure enough—I said something about Cynthia's being a good looking chick and pleasant. I stewed over this, not knowing how to make amends—not only to Cynthia, but to all of womankind—and then I decided to ask Cynthia.

I don't go to the bank that often, because of my impoverished circumstances, and that's one of the things I like about Cynthia. No matter how long since I was in last, Cynthia looks up, her fingers twitching from counting money, and she smiles like a piano keyboard and hails me heartily by name. I like that. It's good to be recognized. I spent over $800 at a store not long ago, and came away leaving my checkbook on the counter, and when I went back for it ten minutes later the clerk didn't know me. But Cynthia never forgets. So I saved money for a time, and when I had a roll of quarters I went in, and Cynthia looked up to smile and call me by name, and I said, "Hi, chick!"

Cynthia's is always the busiest wicket in the bank, which tells us a good deal, and several customers were behind me waiting their turns.

"Hi, yourself," Cynthia said. "Mercy! What makes you so bouncy this morning?"

"Any morning is bouncy in your amiable presence," I said. You can see why I get along with the ladies. Then I added, "Chick."

"You brighten my day too," Cynthia came back, which tells you some more about Cynthia, and then she said, "What gives with this chick stuff?"

"Aren't you mad at me?"

"Mad at you? I'm not mad at anybody. Why should I be mad at you?"

"Because I just called you a chick. I got a letter from a woman who says "chick" is a demeaning word. She says it's bigoted, offensive, degrading, and an open insult to the fair sex. She says I shouldn't call you a chick."

"You bring your money in here, and you can call me Oscar if you want to—call me anything except late for supper!"

(That's a fairly common Maine remark, and is not original with Cynthia—real State-o'-Mainers don't mind what you call 'em so long as you don't call 'em late for supper.)

So I said, "Then may I continue to refer to you as a pleasant and good looking chick?"

"I would if I were you—my grandfather always bounced me on his knee and said I was his little Rhode Island Red pullet. He used to tell me to appreciate it while I could, because sweet little pullets get to be old hens and biddies."

"True, true!" I offered, and I said, "I'd like to withdraw a thousand dollars in twos and threes." Cynthia took my ten-dollar roll of quarters and gave me a deposit slip, and she said, "Eyah."

The ten or fifteen customers now behind me were impatient, so I decided it was time to end this interrogation into the amenities of feminine nomenclature, and I bade Cynthia a fond adieu. She's a sweet chick and lives over at Pleasant Point.

I had another letter at just about the same time from a Ken Blair at 08033, who touched on another deplorable instance of feminine abuse. He said his wife lately made a batch of fudge, which I feel is something no woman should ever do now that they're emancipated, and to punish her for usurping this prerogative he offered to lick the pan clean. He remembered from early boyhood that this was a pleasant way to assist in the making of fudge, and he saw no reason to shirk now that he was a man and his wife would appreciate some help. Myself, I was never much of a fudge licker, but I did enjoy getting the dasher when we froze ice cream. But I was interested in Ken's perplexity because it touched on these new philosophies of sex, gender, and previous condition. Ken says there was nothing to lick. She had used one of these new pots with a Silverstone ® lining, and when she poured the fudge to cool the pot was as clean as a whistle. Ken said the pot looked as if it hadn't been used. Which is just dandy for the pot washer, but what has happened to the rights and privileges of the poor kid, or husband, who likes his fudge lickin's? What right has a woman assumed, in this great battle for supremacy, to use a Silverstone ® pot? And then turn around and complain about what she's called?

45 He Used His Head

Baseball statistics get thrust at us and probably we should all be impressed. One fellow, the radio play-by-play announcer told me with a catch in his throat, was the only left-handed pitcher to strike out nine left-handed batters in an opening night game in St. Louis. The finest sarcasm ever leveled at that kind of frivolous record-keeping is undoubtedly a limerick from the cricket fields of Eton:

> There once was a chappie named Glover
> Who bowled thirty-two wides in one over,
>> Which had never been done
>> By an archdeacon's son
> On a Tuesday in August in Dover.

The worst thing about baseball statistics is their insistence on being big league. Probably 99 percent of all the baseball statistics I regard highly have to do with teams Cooperstown never heard about, and with innocent home-town players who played out-field for some such scrub aggregation as the Second Baptist Sunday School Pirates. Myself, I had my best year with the Unitarians, hitting .201, and this is interesting because while the Unitarian Church still fielded a ball team, the society itself had dissolved twenty years ago. I believe I was the only Congregationalist on the Unversalist team. So why should I get excited over how many home runs Babe Ruth hit?

For example—I was present and saw a catcher make an unassisted triple play, which was even better than that because it made four outs in one inning. It's not in the books, of course. Chubbie Doane was the catcher, and the other team had men on second and third and nobody out. Wagtail Holmes was pitching, and he laid three fastballs right down the pipe for a strike-out. The batter had taken two and was supposed to go to right, and the third-base coach had his men running. Thing is that Chubbie dropped the third strike. He picked the ball up smartly and tagged the batter right in the box, so there was a strike-out for the pitcher and a put-out for Chubbie. Well, the third-base coach lost sight of the ball, somehow, and his two runners kept coming, and Chubbie stood there and tagged them as they came home—one-two, bang-bang. The coach and the runners looked silly enough, but there was Chubbie with the ball in his hand—and it added up to an unassisted triple play and four outs in the inning. So what about Babe Ruth?

Not long ago I was in a supermarket and I found a man looking at the labels on the diet foods. He looked to me like a Bouchard, so I stepped closer and said, "I humbly beg your pardon, and hesitate to intrude while you're reading, but you look to me like a Bouchard." He shifted his focus from a label to my face, and then we broke into grins and shook hands and clapped each other on our backs, and danced up and down. It was Cabot Bouchard, and I hadn't seen him in many a long year. In the 1920s and 1930s he played second base for the Cabot Tigers. As the local journalist, I was official scorer at the games, and I saw Cabot make a play one afternoon that should be in the record books, but it isn't.

In the early days of New England industrialization, the Cabot family of (where else?) Boston invested in what was then known as a "privilege"—the right to generate hydroelectricity for manufacturing purposes. That explains the Cabot Mill at Brunswick, Maine. In its day it was a big cotton maker, and in its later time it pioneered with rayon fabrics. Like all the other New England cotton weavers it sent agents up into French Canada to recruit workers—both men and women. Perhaps it is better to say "girls and boys," because mostly the recruits were young folks off the farms who thought to better themselves. This was "cheap" labor, and by the middle of the 1800s Brunswick had a considerable settlement of such workers. These people held aloof from the Yankee community and kept their own customs, language, and church. The church had a school. It would be long years before much assimilation accrued. Although they kept apart and were unquestionably exploited, these French-Canadians were glad for work in the mills and considered themselves prosperous—at least better off than the relatives still living in Quebec. Cabot Bouchard's mother and father were sentimental about the Cabot Mill, so they named their firstborn Cabot. When Cabot finished the grade classes in St. John's Parochial School and entered Brunswick High, he was already playing good ball and had no trouble making first-string second baseman. Then, when school recessed for the summer, he played the same position on the mill team. That was supposed to be in the semi-pro class, but money wasn't a major matter—the only time I ever played "professionally" I filled in for an outfielder with a broken wrist and they paid me two dollars a game and carfare.

Cabot, as I now encountered him in the grocery store, carries some weight and was not looking at the diet foods for fun. He doesn't stand much over five feet, and when he was playing ball had maybe 140 pounds. Small and light for an athlete, but he was quicker than a pussy cat. He was able to cover a lot of ground and he could turn a double play with ballet grace. It wasn't often a ball went through him, and at the moment I recall he was in his 127th inning without an error. So we stood there and visited and the customers went around us with their carts of groceries, and I mentioned the time he made one of the most sensational plays in the history of baseball. Cabot said he didn't remember it, in particular—no, he said he guessed he'd forgotten all about that one. I never did.

The game was between the Cabot Tigers and the Worumbo Lemons. The Worumbo Mill did pay their players. That is, they'd give a good ball handler a job in the mill as a window oiler or loom lifter, and all he had to do was play ball. Another thing they did was to bring in a ringer on his off day from either the Boston Braves or the Boston Red Sox, and they'd have a big league pitcher named Smith or Jones or Brown. You could get a pitcher like that, then, for $100 and train fare. That should be in the record books, too. Anyway, for this game the Worumbo Lemons had brought up a .300 hitter from Boston, and he came to bat in the bottom of the fourth with the bases loaded and two out. The Cabot Tiger pitcher tried a fast ball, and this paragon from Fenway Park connected with it. It went through the pitcher's box on a streak, so the pitcher never saw it (although afterwards he said he smelled the brimstone) and there was Cabot Bouchard right in front of it and positioned perfectly. Screaming as the ball was, it looked like an easy out for Bouchard, and the end of the threat. But the ball took a crazy bounce so it came up and hit Cabot on his forehead, right at the bridge of his nose, and it laid him out cold on the spot. He slumped as if poleaxed, which is the same thing, and that was that.

The ball could just as well have gone over the fence into the river, but it bounced off Cabot into the air. There was an ungodly bonk!—as if somebody had hit a twelve-quart bucket with a brick. The runner, quite sure he was on with a couple of RBI's, saw Cabot slump, and slowed his pace at sight of what he'd done. Just enough so the first baseman (sees to me in recollection he was a Paiement) had time to catch the ball in the air and make the put-out. As official scorekeeper, it was my function to set all this down in the book, and although Cabot Bouchard was unconscious on the field I had to give him an assist on the play. Then I went out to see if I could help the umpire and the other boys in bringing Cabot around. It took ten or fifteen minutes. A hundred and twenty-seven innings without an error.

That statistic never got the attention it deserved.

46 Pud Lathrop Calls On

Yankee ingenuity has what a professor at the University of Maine most happily described in a bulletin on raspberries as, ". . . a variance within wide limitations." He meant I think, that it comes in all shapes and sizes. One of the shapes, or perhaps one of the sizes, could be illustrated by the truthful tale of Pud Lathrop. I've changed the names here, naturally, but not very much. Principal reason is I wouldn't want Abbie to take offense. It was quite a snowstorm, that one, and I heard that over to East Friendship they got a good two feet, on the level. Mostly, two feet at East Friendship would be a foot and a half anywhere else, so you can believe anybody you want to. After the storm, it was a beautiful morning. The air had subsided and the sun came up golden bright, and the world was handsome to gaze upon. Pud Lathrop stood by his kitchen stove looking out the window down the bay, and the clean serenity quite entranced him—in rapt attention he admired the salubrity. Just before the storm broke, Pud's wife had gone on the bus to Hartford to see the twin grandchildren tackle their tenth birthday, so Pud had weathered the blizzard alone in the big house and he was now making his breakfast. He knew he was snowed in for fair. This would be the big storm of the winter.

His wife would be gone the rest of the week, so there was no great need to get a path shoveled to the road. The pantry was stocked and the freezer was loaded—what's to worry about? Pud cracked four eggs in the yellow bowl with blue stripes and he frothed them. Pud liked a bit of sharp cheese in his scrambled eggs (to give them a pick-wancy) and then he gave 'em some cow. When the sausage had browned and the sweet-potato cakes were crispy at the edge, he'd come back to the eggs. There was an electric toaster on the shelf, but Pud liked his toast made on the top of the hot stove, and he now laid on four slices of bread. Things looked promising. Pud philosophized. Being alone was one thing, but being marooned on top of that was different. He had some bear-paw snowshoes, so he could get out all-right, and then he didn't know as he wanted to get out. The house was quiet, covered with snow, so the steepleclock on the kitchen mantle was knocking instead of ticking and tocking. Pud noticed all at once that he'd turn every minute or so and say something to his wife. Right out loud. Kept forgetting she was in Hartford. Pure habit. Made him feel foolish, but there it was. Then he decided to bake himself a pan of buttermilk biscuits for supper, and by that time the coffee was perking. Why not a steak from the freezer for supper, too? Must take it out to thaw. And fry some onions—with mushrooms. String beans would go good. And must remember to warm the apple pie. No need to plan about noonin' until the time came.

Just up the road, Abbie Pendleton looked out of her kitchen window, and was relieved to see smoke coming from Pud's chimney. "Pud's up and about," she said to her husband. "Leastways, his chimney's smokin'."

"Reasonable assumption," said her husband, whose name is Archibald.

"Snow clearn over his keyholes, looks-if from here," Abbie said.

"He knows he can call on," Archibald said.

So as the forenoon moved along and the afternoon accrued, Abbie looked out now and again towards Pud's house, and smoke from the chimney was the only activity she saw. "Wonder if he's all right," she said.

"He's all right. He knows he can call on."

"Eyah, but he could-da fell or something."

So along about the time Pud was beginning to get ready to slice his onions, his telephone rang. It was Abbie.

"Pud, you all right?"

"Eyah."

"Quite a storm!"

"Eyah, 'twas. Ripper. I'm snowed in for fair. How you doing?"

"Good. Is they anything you need?"

"Guess not. Nothing comes to mind. I'm good. Warm. Plenty to eat. Nothing to do 'cept wait for the wife."

"She comes Friday?"

"No—Sat-dee—less'n the storm keeps her."

"Well, if they's anything you want, call on!"

"Will do."

Next day, Abbie calls again. Pud is fine. Same conversation. "Anything you want, call on!"

"Will do."

But, Pud had begun to react to being alone and doing for himself, and on the fourth morning Pud found himself waiting for Abbie to call. When the telephone rang Pud was ready, and with a big smile he answered, "Tucker's Barber Shop for Dogs and Cats!"

Abbie said, "That you, Pud?"

"Eyah."

"Pud—you all right?"

"Eyah."

"Anything you want?"

"Well, Abbie—yes, they is. I need somebody to tie my bow necktie. Never could do it myself."

"Bow necktie? You dressing up? Going some place?"

"Well, I was sort of expecting that sooner or later you'd get around to asking me over for supper."

47 Mutt of the Finest Kind

Ludwig von Wrincklepuss was a mutt of the finest kind, and a few words about him should cheer people who like dogs. His true parentage was a close secret long lost in the lore of the precinct, and his description would just be that he was a large dog with long legs and enormous feet. His name was offered by Dickie Saunders in a mood of ridicule, for Ludwig was no closer to aristocracy than was archie the cockroach, albeit capitalized. The Ludwig von Wrincklepuss nicked off to "The Baron" almost at once, and The Baron was our family pooch for going-on ten memorable years, attending to every duty with zeal, dispatch, and sagacity. Whatever accrued, there was The Baron, faithful, well in charge, everything in hand, and nothing to worry about. He was loveable to a fault, one of his faults being the cordial wet smack, and let a lady speak to him and he'd come right up in her lap. He loved to meet wayfaring tramps a mile down the road and wagtail them right into our parlor. Of all the dogs we've had, and farm dogs come and go, The Baron was the prince and the pride. I thought so much of him that I faked his papers.

His lineage was accordingly impressive. By Sirius Canis Major out of Cerberus, he had a bounding start, and as his family tree took shape I was apprehensive lest the AKC come around asking questions. An uncle was Argos the Argive, and a first cousin was Gelert of Llewellyn. I recall nearly all of his ancestry: Mother Hubbard's dog, the dogs of war, the little dog that laughed to see such sport, the gingham dog that went bowwow, the dog having his day, his Highness' dog, Hamilcar Barca, the toss'd dog that worried the cat, the dog that bayed the moon, See-nul-nuk (the lead dog on Peary's dash to the Pole), the hound of the Baskervilles, the dog that doth delight to bark and bite, the dog in the manger, Cave Canem, The Fastest Hound Dog In The State Of Maine, dog eat dog, Mad Dogs and Englishmen, snappies and snails, the sleeping dog *(le chien d'or)*, the dog John Bogart bit, and the dog that's always on the wrong side of the door. All these in The Baron's pedigree were too many for the AKC to challenge, so we affixed the notarial seal of our late Justice William F. Bowser (Ret.), together with a blue ribbon, and The Baron's papers were official. No—not *that* AKC; this was the Artificial Kredentials Committee. The Baron's papers came to ten feet and eleven inches.

As the merest pup, he showed great promise. You tell him to do something, and he would do everything he could think of until you told him to stop. He never had to be told a second time, either. He quickly learned to mind the sheep, and also to bring the cows down from pasture. After he brought the cows down, he would go along the tie-up and count them, to be sure he had them all. If one of our best friends chanced in the dooryard, The Baron would growl and hump up and repel the invasion. An uncle who lived with us said one time that we couldn't run the farm without The Baron, but he'd sure like to try. And for some reason the suggestion was made that The Baron should be enrolled and attend an obedience school up to the city that was being advertised in the papers. This seemed droll enough, so on the stated evening the wife took The Baron up to be introduced to the niceties. The Baron was the only mutt. All the other dogs had real papers. Dogpeople wouldn't waste schooling money on a mongrel. The Baron papers didn't impress the lady in charge, and they didn't fool any of the other dogs at all. They looked down their snouts at The Baron in disdain. But this didn't bother The Baron, and he proceeded to make friends in the usual manner. He greeted every dog personally, and then climbed onto the lap of a lady who was fondling a chihuahua. It was impossible not to notice The Baron—he was always so friendly.

When they calmed everything down and attached the leashes, there was some straining among the elite, but not The Baron. The Baron had never seen a leash before, and he thought it was some kind of an honor and a good idea. What The Baron was about to learn at obedience school wasn't much, because he was already able to speak five languages and had a smattering of algebra. The instructors soon saw they didn't need to worry about *him*. They could give all their attention to the high-breds.

The Baron's finest hour came on the last night, during the graduation exercises. Every dog would be taken on his leash and put through his paces, and be judged on his progress during the training. The Baron was all eager for this. And just then some naughty boys passed by and hove a volunteer pussy-cat in the window so it landed close to all the dogs who were to be graduated. The cat treed on a piano. All the obedient dogs gave this matter their full attention. All except The Baron. The Baron knew that baiting our barn cats back home was a no-no, and from his earliest puppy days he had stinging memories of what it is like when a tomcat climbs aboard and rides a puppy down into the woodlot. Pins and needles. The Baron thus stood in calm composure and watched the bedlam, the hullabaloo, the hooraw. There could be no second in the obedience trials that night. The judges had no choice. The Baron took home the big blue rosette. He stood there immobile, completely uninterested, needing no instructions whatever.

The Baron was petrified of cats.

48 And Far Afield

"**H**ebdomadal" is a good word, and should give any essay a classy start. And how about *Kaiserschmarrn*? That's a good word, too. Our hebdomadal newspaper has just printed a recipe for *Kaiserschmarrn*. I was no more surprised to find a recipe for *Kaiserschmarrn* than you were to bump into hebdomadal. All this is far afield, indeed. *Kaiserschmarrn* has been translated as "emperor's pancake" and Austria and Bavaria dispute which originated it. Years ago I enjoyed *Kaiserschmarrn* in one of the little red *Speisewagens* of the German Federal Railroad, where for a long time it has been the traditional dessert for the dining traveler. I have no idea if the *Kaiserschmarrn* is eaten otherwise, and I never had one except on a train. When I first met a *Kaiserschmarrn*, I thought the waiter was overly insistent, even pushy about it, but I didn't know I was expected to have one willy-nilly just because I was dining on a train. Following a considerable preparation, the cook carefully mixes numerous ingredients, and comes up with a pancake that is torn apart with two forks and served with a jelly—a *Konfiture*. Not too many Germans would know what maple syrup is. And as the cook takes his time compounding the *Kaiserschmarrn*, the waiter serves it gallantly with all the fuss and flourish of something *en flambeau* at a French restaurant in The Village. Big deal! However, a *Kaiserschmarrn* is a delicious dessert and who has had one in a little red *Speisewagen* will treasure the memory forever.

The recipe in our hebdomadal newspaper is, I insist, by no means a good one. It is too simple. Maybe it's close, though:

KAISERSCHMARRN
(Emperor's Pancake)

8 eggs
2 cups plus 2 Tablespoons milk
Salt
1½ cups flour
Raisins
Confectioner's sugar
Plum jelly

Separate eggs. Combine yolks with milk, salt, and flour to form paste. Beat egg whites until stiff and fold into batter. Stir in raisins. Melt 2 tablespoons of butter or margarine in a heavy 8-inch skillet. Fry pancake on both sides, and break with two forks into 6 or 8 pieces. Sprinkle with confectioner's sugar and serve with plum jelly.

Which is all right, except that, for a starter, I don't see any vanilla. Years after I was back in Maine after my visit to West Germany, my own good cook, who knew nothing about a *Kaiserschmarrn*, and I visited the interesting port of Churchill far up in Canada's Manitoba, on Hudson Bay. There is no highway to Churchill, and flying depends day-to-day on the curious Hudson Bay weather, so the right way to reach Churchill is by railroad. At that time the Canadian National Railway train departed Winnipeg, and reached Churchill in three days after two sleeps. This was the first time I had stepped into a railway dining car since I had returned from West Germany.

The dining car had a West Indian steward who gave us every care. The food was excellent, the table beautiful with linen, crystal, silver, and china. On our first evening out of Winnipeg we were still in prairie land—the permafrost was still well ahead. It was July, so the sun ran along the horizon in midnight sun fashion, rather than dropping over the edge. We lingered, and when we started for our sleeping compartment in another car we passed the entrance into the kitchen. There was the cook and his assistant in white, with chef's caps, and the usual smell of a kitchen. "Fine supper!" I called. "Thank you!" The chef turned to look at me, smiled, and thanked me in an accent that couldn't be missed.

"Deutscher!" I said. His name was Richard Horn, and he was a Swabian, from Stuttgart. He had been a soldier, and as a POW had been interned in Alabama. At the end of the war he hoped to stay in the United States, but he couldn't bring this off and went to Canada, instead. Before the war he had been a cook in a red *Speisewagen* of the German Federal Railway, and what more reasonable than cooking for the Canadian National? Only those who have been to Germany will appreciate how we stood there in the doorway of the kitchen and shook hands as only those who have been to Germany can. Shaking hands is the second biggest sport in Germany. Eating is first, and third is soccer. When we said good night to Herr Horn I said, "So, tomorrow for supper, we'll have a *Kaiserschmarrn!*"

And we did. And it certainly was farther afield than the recipe in our hebdomadal newspaper. When we came into the dining car our steward seated us, and with an air of confidence he said, "I don't know what's going on, but Cook has pots and pans laid out all over the place!"

"He's making us a *Kaiserschmarrn*," I told him.

He said, "You don't say!"

When dessert time came, our steward was completely at a loss about serving a *Kaiserschmarrn*, so Herr Horn came in to do that. He deftly rent the pancake apart, tossed it neatly, and laid the pieces on our plates. He put on the *Konfiture*, and apologized because the commissary of the Canadian National Railways had not foreseen his need and had not supplied vanilla beans. "Without vanilla sugar, where are you?" he asked.

Well, we were something like a thousand miles north of Winnipeg, closer to The Pas than to any other town. The Pas is the junction where the railroad to Flin Flon takes off. We were in permafrost country. But for all that, we could well have been somewhere in the Swabian Alps, just out of Stuttgart headed for Munich. Except, that is, except for vanilla beans.

The other passengers—the other diners—became interested, and Herr Horn made *Kaiserschmarrn* that evening for everybody. It's entirely possible *Kaiserschmarrn* became customary on the Churchill line of the CPR. We haven't been back to see, but by now they'd have vanilla beans.

49 Here's to the Old Geezers!

A letter to the editor objected with asperity to calling us old geezers geezers, and thus the refinements of vastly improved semantics career along in hot pursuit of something or other. I read this letter just after I had heard from another old geezer, a friend from my youth (and his) who had just lately organized his "Friendly Society of Old Geezers," meant to counteract the lah-de-dah of "Senior Citizens." He asked if I cared to join, and I joined at once. Members of the Friendly Society of Old Geezers are asked to report (among other things) instances where city engineers raise the level of curbstones without placing announcements in the papers. As a true and undaunted, and now accredited, Old Geezer, I don't trip over too many elevated curbstones out here in the rural precinct, but I can say that now and then I step to my workbench to get a tool and can't remember which one. But I am in no way offended at Old Geezer and smile when some pipsqueak calls me The Ancient Mariner and sometimes Old Duffer. I am also on record as opposed to custodian for janitor, security officer for night watchman, and communications consultant for tub thumper.

The writer of that letter to the editor reveals that he / she (that's a people-person) doesn't know that "geezer" is a friendly word. And I don't think "senior citizen" is friendly. The crabby, crotchety, hard-to-get-along-with, nose-out-of-joint, chip-on-his-shoulder buzzard down the road is never called a geezer. An old crab, maybe, or a character, or a nut, or a skinflint, but never an old geezer. Geezers are nice people. A plain citizen may be nice or not nice, but he's just a run-of-the-mill individual, neither hay nor grass, and comparable in the aggregate to, say, taxpayers, denizens, residents, boxholders, customers, and even the "patrons" who mail letters at the post office. A senior citizen, otherwise human, is no more than an elderly "young squirt"—showing promise, but . . .

Our language, give it credit, has many a good word like geezer until "senior citizen" is unneeded. How about "cuss"? First, a cuss has to be old—there is no young cuss. A young cuss would be a whippersnapper, perhaps. A gentleman who has grown up with the vernacular isn't offended; "Who's the old cuss with the goatee?" "Cuss," like "geezer," is always positive; "He's a fine old cuss of the first water!" Or, "Now, you take that Harry—he's a comical old cuss!"

A word that might replace geezer is "thing." But thing, at times, can be bisexual; "She's a persnickety thing!" or, "He's a dear old thing—I take him cookies every time I bake." A true geezer won't care what you call him if you bring him cookies. "Rig" is about like thing; "She's a rig, that one!" or, "You talk about a rig, that's him!" But rigs aren't always old; "He was a comical rig away back in school!"

Another thing people who write letters to the editor need to understand is the way we (at least here in Maine) abuse somebody when we're being pleasant. Anybody from away may misunderstand. Like "reprobate." If we had any reprobates in Maine they'd be hurt if somebody called them reprobates. But some sweet, kindly, loveable old geezer noted for his constant and hearty good cheer and his kind words and deeds, and his good manners, can be greeted with, "Why Henry! You disreputable old reprobate—where've you been? Ain't seen you in ages! Are you out for good?" Henry, naturally, is not only pleased, but honored by such complimentary imputation. He belongs. Such discourse sets him apart, as would an honorary degree. Some other words used in Maine with the same left-handed kindness are "skinflint," "backslider," "rascal," "hossthief," "shyster," "Democrat," "rapscallion," "hairpin" (crooked!), "poacher," and "goat." "Hey, you old goat, good to see you!" And most congenial people who will readily rally to these opprobrious terms will get huffy if you call them senior citizens. By the way, a geezer and a jeezer are not the same. In Aroostock and Washington Counties, Mainers like the word "jeezer." "This jeezer comes along . . ." It doesn't mean anything one way or the other, except that a jeezer would be male, and mature. He may also be old. The origin of this is unknown, and the way "jeezer" is used it's doubtful if it ever derived from "geezer." As said, "geezer" is a friendly word, but "jeezer" doesn't have to be.

Stet Plummer used to say, back when he was not quite in the geezer range, that if he had something rammed down his throat (i.e., *throurt*) even if it was good he didn't like it. It seems to me that "senior citizen" has been rammed down our throurts in a quick decision that wasn't given enough thought. The language has plenty of better ways to say it. And, I don't believe old people, who are supposed to be the sensitive ones in this connection, are basically offended by being old. Years ago, when the Boston *Post* was flourishing (it ceased publishing in the 1950s) the editorial page had what was called "the list of spry old New Englanders." Anybody reaching eighty and in reasonable health could expect to be added to that list, and it was an honor. The *Post* was an unusual paper, even in those days, and there was a comical line that used to appear regularly in the little notes about Spry Old New Englanders. Other newspapers would report on a, say, ninetieth birthday and report, "He is hale and hearty and able to read the Bible without glasses." In the *Post* this line always read, ". . . and able to read the Boston *Post* without glasses." It was certainly not undignified in those days to be added to the *Post*'s list of old people. It was the *Post* that thought up the promotional gimmick of giving a gold-headed cane to the oldest man in town. These canes were, and still are, handed along through the generations. So time was that the "old folks" had their place and their honors with all the comfy good will they deserved, rocking chairs and soft slippies and grandchildren on their laps for the Red Riding Hood sessions. Warm and cozy, and no chip on the shoulder. Twilight, and evensong, and leisure and repose. The senior citizen, who has replaced the old geezers, is getting his "benefits" and you see him at the bank on the third day of every month. He gets discounts at hotels and on buses and planes, and the chain stores give him a wallet card so he can get 10 percent at any branch. The senior citizen may be better off—who's to say? But he lacks the chummy quality of the one-time old codger—the cuss, the joker, the rig, and all good old geezers everywhere who are satisfied to be themselves.

My friend who organized the Friendly Society of Old Geezers writes that one of life's dearest moments is when the comely young babe on the bus stands up to offer you her seat.

50 And Funny About That, Too

Somebody asked me why I'd never done a report on "Shine" Fauchette. Just oversight; I hadn't forgotten Shine, because once you saw him you'd never forget him. Last I heard he was guiding for bear up around New Vineyard somewhere, and doing all right, but come to think of it, that was years ago now. Shine belongs with the best of them in Maine lumbering lore. He came after the big days of the Bangor Tigers, who specialized in river driving and never cared how a river raged, but he was of that stripe and could have held his own with them. Shine was still at his peak when the Maine timberland people gave up the spring drives and began building roads and using trucks. Shine was a "P-I," which means a Prince Edward Islander. Came from a little place called Crapaud, between Borden and Charlottetown, and when he was eighteen he came down to the Boston States to find work. His front name was Roland—Roland Fauchette. He signed up with Ned O'Neill as one of the 140 men who built the big camp at Haymock Pond and drove the East Branch. Ned was fabulous, too—one of the real old-time bosses. He liked the looks of Roland Fauchette at first sight, and he said to Leo Thibodeau, the hiring boss, "You watch that boy—he'll make his mark!" Strapping lad; two ax handles at the shoulders, and handsome to boot. Straight as a spruce. He had double teeth.

Fact. That's very unusual. All the way around, upper and lower, he had perfect double teeth, strong and good. But at that time nobody knew that he had double teeth. Roland Fauchette went in with the first bunch and helped clear the place and put up the buildings, and everything was ready for the rest of the men by the time there came a snatch of snow for sledding and they could team in supplies. That was a big camp, and it took several day to sled in everything from the depot farm at Kokadjo, and come night every man jack was worn out from lugging and unpacking and putting on shelves. All except Roland Fauchette—he'd go all day long, right out straight, and never tucker one bit. Big and rugged. Something to see, he was. And the third morning, in comes a double sled loaded with hogsheads of dry peas—the pea soup sled. A hogshead of anything is something to handle, and the men weren't looking forward to getting these off the sled and rolled into the storehouse. But Roland Fauchette walks over to the back of the sled and pulls the fid on the chain around the load, and he stoops over and clamps his teeth right onto the chime end of a hogshead, and he lifts the thing right up, 'thout touching it with his hands at all, and he turns and sets it down on the snow and then goes back to get a second one.

Well, sir—Ned O'Neill sees Roland Fauchette do this, and he came right over. "I seen it," he says, "and I don't believe it!"

"Seen what?" says Roland Fauchette.

"I seen you pick up a hogshead of peas with your teeth!"

"Aye," says Roland Fauchette. "Easiest way."

"How can you do that?"

"I got double teeth."

Well at that every man in camp has to come over and look at Roland's teeth, and then they stood back and watched him pick those hogsheads off the sled and set them down, and as nobody had ever seen anything like that before, there was considerable talk about it.

It was funny about that. Roland Fauchette, having double teeth, used twice as much tooth powder as anybody else. Fact is that because he took extra special care of his double teeth he used even more. So along in February, going on March, Roland Fauchette runs out of tooth powder. In a camp like that you don't just step down the street and buy things. Snow over the eaves; you wait for spring. The cockshop didn't have any tooth paste, and the best the clerk could do was promise some for next winter. This is where Milo Gagnon comes in. Milo took care of the horses. And he remembered that he had some powder in a can on a shelf. The next morning Roland brushed, and it turned out this powder wasn't tooth powder at all, as Milo thought, but something for shining brass on harnesses and polishing team bells. Upshot was, Roland Fauchette's double teeth turned a bright phosphorescent tangerine color, so when he came for breakfast he looked like a gallon of orange paint. The stuff had cleaned his teeth all right, and that part was good, because he never had to clean them again. That's how Roland Fauchette came to be called Shine.

Of all the stories that came to be told about Shine Fauchette and his double teeth, the one I like best is after hours. When the big lamp was blown out and the men settled down in the bunkhouse for a night's sleep, Shine would pull his blanket over his head, open his mouth, and read a book.